This book honors the memory of Ralph Brian Perry,
who lost his life in a helicopter crash on February 10, 1986,
while on assignment to photograph Mount St. Helens.

ENDPAPERS: *Juggernaut from the sea sweeps
terrified victims to a watery grave in a
Japanese wood-block print of 1896. The
tsunami depicted, one of the worst in
recorded history, claimed 27,000 lives as
towering waves slammed into the Sanriku
coast of northeastern Honshu. Soon after
the disaster, news stories prompted an
outpouring of contributions for the relief of
the survivors. This print appeared in a
magazine specially prepared to report on
the catastrophe.*

KOKUSHO KANKOKAI, INC.

ONCE SUBMERGED, A LIFELESS TREE RISES ABOVE THE PARCHED BED OF A RESERVOIR DURING THE AUSTRALIAN DROUGHT OF 1983.

NATURE ON THE RAMPAGE
Our Violent Earth

Prepared by the Special Publications Division
National Geographic Society, Washington, D.C.

NATURE ON THE RAMPAGE: *Our Violent Earth*
Contributing Authors: RON FISHER, TOM MELHAM,
CYNTHIA RUSS RAMSAY, GENE S. STUART

Published by THE NATIONAL GEOGRAPHIC SOCIETY
GILBERT M. GROSVENOR, *President*
MELVIN M. PAYNE, *Chairman of the Board*
OWEN R. ANDERSON, *Executive Vice President*
ROBERT L. BREEDEN, *Senior Vice President,*
  Publications and Educational Media

Prepared by THE SPECIAL PUBLICATIONS DIVISION
DONALD J. CRUMP, *Director*
PHILIP B. SILCOTT, *Associate Director*
BONNIE S. LAWRENCE, *Assistant Director*
MARY ANN HARRELL, *Consulting Editor*

Staff for this Book
MARGERY G. DUNN, *Managing Editor*
JOHN G. AGNONE, *Illustrations Editor*
JODY BOLT, *Art Director*
CAROLINDA E. HILL, *Project Coordinator and*
  Senior Researcher
MONIQUE F. EINHORN, TEE LOFTIN, BRUCE G. NORFLEET,
  Researchers
MELISSA L. FLY, SUSANNE E. FRÜH, *Research Assistants*
LESLIE B. ALLEN, SEYMOUR L. FISHBEIN, RON FISHER,
  TOM MELHAM, *Picture Legend Writers*
SUSAN SANFORD, *Map Art and Illustrations*
SHARON KOCSIS BERRY, STUART E. PFITZINGER,
  Illustrations Assistants

Engraving, Printing, and Product Manufacture
ROBERT W. MESSER, *Manager*
GEORGE V. WHITE, *Assistant Manager*
DAVID V. SHOWERS, *Production Manager*
GEORGE J. ZELLER, JR., *Production Project Manager*
GREGORY STORER, *Senior Assistant*
  Production Manager
MARK R. DUNLEVY, *Assistant Production Manager*
TIMOTHY H. EWING, *Production Assistant*

VICKI L. BROOM, CAROL ROCHELEAU CURTIS,
  MARY ELIZABETH DAVIS, ROSAMUND GARNER,
  ARTEMIS S. LAMPATHAKIS, SANDRA F. LOTTERMAN,
  ELIZA C. MORTON, CLEO E. PETROFF, VIRGINIA A.
  WILLIAMS, *Staff Assistants*

STEPHANY J. FREEDMAN, *Indexer*

RIGHT: TORNADO TOUCHES DOWN NEAR CORDELL, OKLAHOMA.
PAGES 2-3: ALASKA'S AUGUSTINE VOLCANO ERUPTS IN 1986.
HARDCOVER: LIGHTNING STRIKES ARIZONA'S TUCSON MOUNTAINS.

UNIVERSITY OF MISSISSIPPI / NSSL / NOAA (RIGHT); STEVEN C. KAUFMAN (PAGES 2-3);
TOM IVES (HARDCOVER)

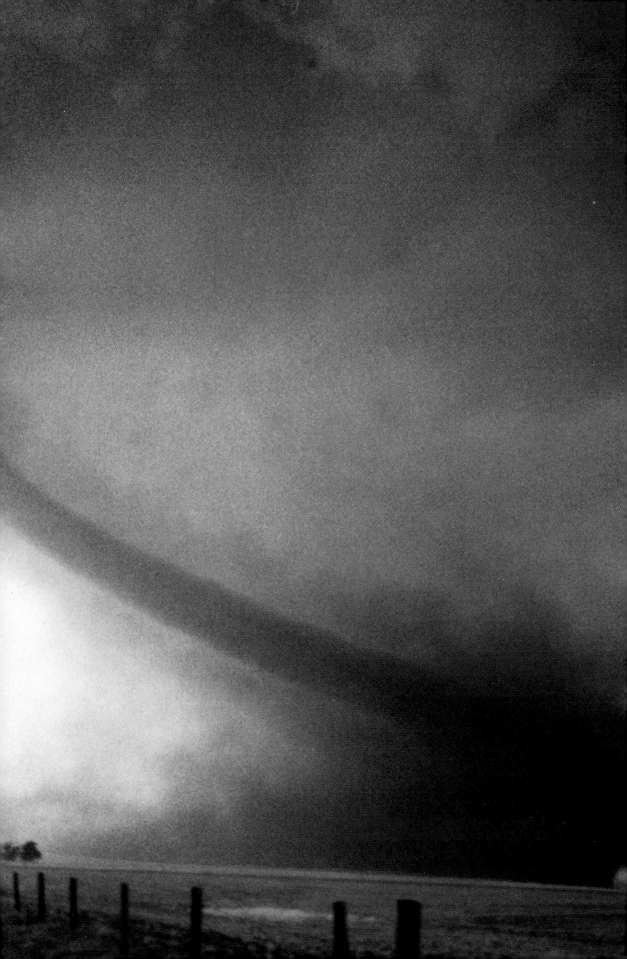

AFTER THE STATE'S WORST FLOODING EVER, IN NOVEMBER 1985, CLEANUP BEGINS IN ROWLESBURG, WEST VIRGINIA.

Foreword

by *Gilbert F. White*
Distinguished Professor Emeritus of Geography
The University of Colorado at Boulder

Extreme events in nature attract special interest because of their dramatic violence and the human suffering they often inflict. Most of these events—the raging storm, the seismic shock, the lightning strike—cannot be controlled. Only a few, such as some floods or pest invasions, can be mitigated. Yet the human consequences may be affected drastically by human actions before or during the episode.

Great physical and biological disturbances are normal. They are part of natural systems, and many perform essential functions. This book graphically presents the power of these events and the ways in which they disrupt or destroy people's lives. It also suggests that beyond the grandeur and drama lie two absorbing challenges.

One challenge is to probe the natural processes at work. It is important, for example, to be able to estimate where the extremes will occur. Earthquake zones, floodplains, storm surge zones, and other areas at risk need to be identified. It is also desirable to predict when the events will occur. So far, forecasting the peak of a flash flood or the landfall of a tropical cyclone is very difficult, but it often is much more practicable than predicting an earthquake or the onset of a drought.

The other major challenge is to design and carry out measures that will alleviate human distress. Warning systems can alert people in the path of destruction. Evacuation procedures can guide them to safety. Buildings can be constructed to minimize earthquake damage. Land use can be planned to avoid uneconomic exposure to landslides or floods. Farmers can adopt practices making them less subject to losses from hail or drought or pests.

These and other measures call for careful scientific and engineering research and for skillful application by informed individuals or government bodies. We shall never be able to eliminate completely the hazard of losses from extreme events; but where life is at stake or heavy losses could be averted at reasonable cost, we should not be satisfied unless serious steps are taken to reduce the risks. The need is especially urgent in developing regions in transition from folk to industrial societies; they are highly susceptible to disruptions from drought, earthquake, flood, or disease.

The tasks of estimating vulnerability and applying practical measures illustrate three fundamental themes in geography that help us see the picture whole. An area's location sets the broad physical limits within which different events may occur. Each place has its distinctive combination of physical and human characteristics shaping the hazards to which it is vulnerable. The evolving interaction of people and environment in each place affects the opportunities and the costs that the rampaging forces of nature will reap.

Huddled against an inferno of dust and heat, women of Rajasthan, India, pray for the relief of monsoon rains in June 1983. Their advent, on the heels of the searing rohini, *or dry period, occasions joy and thanksgiving. But their failure, every few years, augurs crop loss and even famine.*

Fortitude in the face of catastrophe: Members of a Mexican family gather amid the rubble of their adobe home in Ciudad Guzman after the devastating earthquake of September 1985. Survivors of natural calamity—often impoverished already—confront the burdensome task of rebuilding their lives. Where do they begin? Researchers answer: with a spirit of self-reliance that attests human resilience. Disaster victims tend to turn first to family and friends for assistance; if these prove inadequate or unavailable, they seek help from relief agencies. In 1985, international relief organizations had their busiest year ever.

FOLLOWING PAGES: Piton de la Fournaise—Furnace Peak—of Réunion island spews molten lava into the Indian Ocean during an eruption in March 1986. Recalling biblical accounts of cataclysm, such fiery events in fact have shaped our planet from its beginning. Scientists say most of the earth's crust, and perhaps the primitive atmosphere and the oceans as well, came into being through volcanic activity.

PIERRE PERRIN / SYGMA (FOLLOWING PAGES)

Acts of God, Acts of Man

by Tom Melham

*"...and, lo, there was
a great earthquake;
and the sun became black
as sackcloth of hair;
and the moon
became as blood;*

*And the stars of heaven
fell unto the earth,
even as a fig tree
casteth her untimely figs,
when she is shaken
of a mighty wind.*

*And the heaven
departed as a scroll
when it is rolled together;
and every mountain
and island were moved
out of their places."*

—Revelation 6:12-14

Thus says the Book of Revelation, that apocalyptic vision of the future in which the forces of good struggle with the forces of evil and eventually prevail. For his powerful imagery, the prophet draws heavily on nature's wilder aspects: In addition to earthquakes, he describes catastrophic plagues and pestilences, falling stars and hailstorms, booming thunderclaps and lightning flashes, a burning mountain and a lake of fire. As the old order is destroyed to usher in the new, divine might is revealed in the violence of nature.

Before biblical times and since, nature has generated enormous mystery and fear, its awesome powers often eclipsing man's comprehension as well as his physical achievements. The parting and closing of the waters in Exodus 14, some scholars say, may have resulted from seismic sea waves known as tsunami—in which case it was a stunning demonstration of natural might. So was the eruption of Mount Vesuvius that blanketed Pompeii and Herculaneum with suffocating ash and gases in A.D. 79, bringing both cities not only annihilation but also immortality. The Black Death that ravaged medieval Europe claimed millions of lives—possibly one of every three people then on the Continent!

Nature's rampages in the Book of Revelation should not surprise us. In fact many religions describe such apocalyptic visions, while virtually all faiths have at some time explained the violent excesses of nature as punishments inflicted by an angry deity. How else could man—God's chosen creature in monotheistic religions—accept his vulnerability to the earthquakes, storms, and other tumultuous forces that, without warning, repeatedly humbled his grandest works? To him, nature was mysterious, powerful, uncontrollable.

But ours is a different age, one in which spacecraft and electron microscopes routinely probe the largest and smallest of natural realms. Remote sensing now helps us dissect by deduction objects we cannot even see, such as the sun's interior or a tiny virus. We can reroute rivers, obliterate mountains, monitor the world's weather, and engineer vaccines against once dread diseases. We have made ourselves healthier, longer-lived, and more powerful than any previous generation. Unfortunately, we are already redesigning nature by accident; if pollution and other unintended abuses can so easily alter earth's atmosphere and oceans—vastnesses so huge we long thought them immune to our influences— what might our concerted and deliberate efforts achieve? We now talk of harnessing volcanic energy and of predicting or even preventing major earthquakes.

But consider that earthquakes still topple modern cities as surely as they leveled ancient Knossos and Rhodes. That famine—one of the Four Horsemen of the Apocalypse—continues to overtake millions today, especially in parts of Africa. That biological plagues as old as locusts and as contemporary as AIDS still rack the world, even these modern United States. That although we now realize why and how volcanoes erupt, we cannot delay or defuse their eruptions, or even predict most of them with certainty.

Even so, we are learning more every year. We now know that most powers of nature stem from a common source—heat. Two heat systems warm the earth, one fired externally by the solar furnace, the other internally by the planet's radioactive elements, which give off energy as they decay. From either source, heat builds unequally, creating currents in air, water, or even the rocks of the earth's mantle. Solar energy sets up evaporation, winds, storms, droughts, and all other manifestations of weather, while earth's internal heat causes continental drift and associated events such as eruptions, earthquakes, and landslides. We think we understand these general mechanisms—but we can neither control nor change them. When challenged by one of the earth's climatic or tectonic upheavals, we continue to respond much as ancient man did—we flee. Evacuations may be more orderly now, but their success still hinges on accurate forecasting—and modern forecasts consist of possibilities, not sure things.

In May 1985, for example, the U.S. Geological Survey warned that Mount St. Helens could erupt explosively within a matter of days; while small amounts of lava did ooze to the surface, there was no major eruption. Grim weather forecasts in September moved Washington, D.C., to barricade its monuments and itself in anticipation of the "storm of the century"— Hurricane Gloria—which then proceeded to skirt the capital (and most of the East Coast). That same year, two major earthquakes within 36 hours devastated Mexico City, and two others leveled mountain villages in Chile and small towns in Tajikistan in the Soviet Union; all of them caught the inhabitants unprepared.

Also in 1985: Two tropical cyclones ravaged Bangladesh, one killing perhaps ten thousand people overnight; Indonesian volcanoes forced entire island populations to evacuate; a snowcapped cone in Colombia erupted, triggering vast mudflows that buried 23,000 inhabitants; typhoon-related floods left two million homeless in China; forest fires ignited by lightning blackened hundreds of thousands of acres in the

American West. And what of those haunt-ingly emaciated Sudanese and Ethiopians, thousands of whom succumbed that year to starvation and disease?

Then in August 1986: Lethal gases were released from a volcanic lake in Cameroon, asphyxiating some 1,500 villagers in the night. It seems that in spite of all our accumulated knowledge and expertise, all our globe-girdling networks of computer-ized satellites and seismographs, all our scientific theories, all our agricultural, medical, and technological breakthroughs, nature still surprises and overpowers us.

One reason is simply that nature oper-ates on such a gigantic scale; a single major volcanic eruption can unleash the com-bined energy of thousands of atomic bombs. Even 20th-century man cannot re-strain such natural muscle. Nor are we always adept at deciphering nature's intri-cacies. Weather, for example, commands a global front; meteorological events in one place can dramatically alter conditions continents away.

Take the climatic phenomenon called *El Niño*—The Child—because of its ten-dency to develop at Christmastime. Most years, El Niño remains strictly local, marked by a brief reversal of ocean cur-rents off western South America and affecting the weather and the fish pop-ulations of northern Peru or Ecuador. But the 1982-83 Niño turned into a monster. It was the largest and most destructive one on record, spawning prolonged storms, wrong-way trade winds, and quirky weather throughout three-fourths of the world. Millions of seabirds and fish disap-peared from their normal haunts. The huge anchovy fishery off Peru was drasti-cally depleted. Weather systems went into reverse or migrated thousands of miles, in-undating deserts and desiccating lush re-gions. Floods beset parts of North and South America—while droughts ravaged the Philippines, Indonesia, southern Afri-ca, Australia, and parts of India. Hurri-canes roiled the normally calm south-central Pacific. Mud slides buried Peruvian villages and carted off chunks of the Pan-American Highway in Ecuador.

El Niño was also blamed, sometimes unjustly, for a slew of secondary events that included encephalitis outbreaks in the east-ern United States (wet weather there en-couraged mosquitoes to breed), increased shark attacks off Oregon, and giant kelp die-offs along the coast of southern Califor-nia (both linked to unseasonably warm waters). At last count, this destructive, 18-month aberration in the global climate sys-tem had brought about more than a thousand human deaths and some eight billion dollars' worth of damages. Meteo-rologists failed to see it coming or to pre-dict its far-flung effects; many later admitted that numerous signs—subtle warmings of ocean waters, abrupt rises and drops in atmospheric pressures, un-usual calms—had been detected but dis-counted because they didn't fit the usual seasonal pattern of El Niño evolution.

Ultimately, however, the responsibility for the severity of most natural catastro-phes lies not with the forecasters, or even with nature; it lies with us. For though we cannot prevent these events from occur-ring, we can almost always mitigate their ill effects. Instead we often make them worse. We may call them "natural disas-ters" and "acts of God," but our own acts can increase their destructiveness. A flood or a mudflow, for instance, becomes a di-saster when people live in its path.

Consider the heavily publicized drought and famine that have laid waste the African Sahel in recent years. A region-al lack of rain—a circumstance of nature—triggered initial crop failures, but rainfall has long since returned to normal levels in many areas. Evidence gathered by scientif-ic and relief agencies indicates that today's famine persists not so much from pro-longed drought as from prolonged abuses of land and water resources. Greatly inten-sified farming and grazing practices here are taxing the region beyond its capacity to rebound. Water tables have fallen drasti-cally, sapped by too many wells and by ex-tensive deforestation for fuel—which also contributes to severe erosion. The continu-ing loss of humus reduces not only the soil's fertility but also its ability to retain water;

increased runoff results, further accelerating erosion and keeping the land parched even in wet seasons. The continuing desertification of the Sahel is largely a man-caused phenomenon.

So was the transformation of parts of the American West, which began just over a century ago. Far drier than the East, western regions nevertheless had for millennia drawn enough rain to support grasslands. But in the late 19th and early 20th centuries severe overgrazing, combined with local dry spells, destroyed the sod's tough root systems, permitting the fertile soil to blow away—while the drought-resistant sagebrush was allowed to dominate the range. More recently, farmers have overcultivated drier areas of Haiti, India, the Andean nations, and the Central Asian steppes, undercutting future productivity.

Drought currently ranks as the world's worst natural disaster in terms of the number of people affected. According to the U.S. Office of Foreign Disaster Assistance (USOFDA), droughts victimized some 18.5 million people a year during the 1960s; the figure reached 24.4 million in the '70s. And halfway through the '80s there were reports of up to 30 million annually, *in Africa alone.* Are we witnessing a sudden, inexplicable global drying out? Many experts don't think so. Rather, people in many parts of the world are working marginal lands ever harder—to the detriment of those lands and of their own futures. Interestingly, although drought touches more people than any other natural disaster, it is flooding that constitutes our fastest-growing natural hazard. USOFDA data show that the number of flood victims nearly tripled from 5.2 million annually in the 1960s to 15.4 million the next decade.

Increasingly, the most severely affected areas are also the poorest; those Third World nations with struggling economies and exploding populations find themselves plagued with more and more natural disasters, so much so that in those countries such calamities often have political consequences. According to some observers, famine in Ethiopia helped ignite the revolution that overthrew Haile Selassie in

1974. Four years earlier a tropical cyclone and accompanying storm surge slammed into East Pakistan, killing perhaps half a million people. Inadequate response to the disaster by the national leaders a thousand miles away in West Pakistan led to a civil war and eventual independence for East Pakistan, now known as Bangladesh.

*O*f all natural threats, storms should be among the least likely to catch us off guard. Storms are visible—unlike the deep churnings of magma, or the locust eggs that hatch out underground in plague proportions. Weather satellites continuously monitor storm development and position, while weather stations gather surface data that help gauge a storm's intensity. Also, storms often tend to be regional, frequenting some areas far more than others. Knowing this, we can choose to avoid tornado alleys and hurricane zones as homesites, or we can prepare ourselves to cope with a location's inherent hazards. Or we can accept the risks and take our chances.

That is what people have done in Bangladesh, a country poised on the Ganges-Brahmaputra Delta at the head of the Bay of Bengal. Like the Caribbean, the bay seasonally experiences hurricanes—locally called cyclones. These tropical storms often head northward into the funnel-shaped bay and then toward heavily populated Bangladesh. Also, because the bay rapidly narrows and shallows out to the north, sea waves associated with these storms often increase dramatically in size and destructiveness as they approach land. Add to this the fact that the country, being deltaic, is flat and extremely low-lying, and one can see why it is so vulnerable to cyclone and flood damage.

Cyclones are a fact of life here, as are the rich soil and steamy climate. Nature has also given Bangladesh a hundred or so chars—muddy coastal islets, miles wide but often only inches above sea level. Born of silt dropped as the slowing rivers meet the bay, the chars periodically shift in size and shape according to prevailing currents and winds. Their offshore location guarantees they will receive the brunt of any

High-water genesis: A storm surge begins to take shape beneath a hurricane's center, where extremely low atmospheric pressure causes the ocean to rise in a watery dome often 50 miles wide and several feet high. Powerful onshore winds whip up even higher swells and storm waves. As the hurricane heads for land, the shallowing seafloor slows down approaching waves, causing them to pile up and greatly amplifying their heights. Thus the dome, inconspicuous at sea, comes ashore as a devastating wall of water (diagram) with battering waves that can splinter boats or

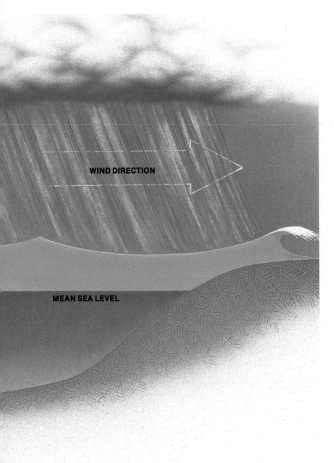

WIND DIRECTION

MEAN SEA LEVEL

cyclone that comes their way. Despite their vulnerability, however, tens of thousands of people live on them.

With a population nearly half that of the United States, the Wisconsin-size nation of Bangladesh does not have the luxury of letting its chars lie fallow. They may be little more than unstable, sea-level mud flats, but they can be extremely fertile. Newborn chars mean opportunity for the country's landless millions, who dream of carving out individual homesteads—even though most of them will remain sharecroppers in a nation where landowners are generally few and relatively rich. Almost as soon as these minimal islets arise from the bay, peasants from the mainland and nearby chars and islands rush to plant them in rice and to pasture out cattle—although they know the chars will continue to shift and that cyclones inevitably will hit. They also know that without using such lands, they and their families might starve.

In May 1985 a moderately strong cyclone retraced the path of the 1970 storm, and another 10,000 char dwellers were swept to their deaths. One of the worst-hit places was Urir Char, the home of seven or eight thousand squatters.

Ironically, Bangladesh had by that time acquired a storm-tracking and storm-predicting system that was the equal of any in the world. Officials in Dhaka, the nation's capital, accurately monitored the cyclone's approach and broadcast warnings, which were relayed by thousands of Red Cross volunteers in the coastal area. Though they knew the storm was coming, Urir Char's squatters decided to ride it out. Even if the warnings had been heeded, many people probably still would have drowned, for transportation to and from Urir Char is extremely limited even in good

houses—and wash away the unwary. Worldwide, nine out of ten hurricane deaths stem from storm surge rather than high-velocity winds or heavy rains; increased public awareness of this hazard, timely warnings, and evacuation of low-lying areas can sharply reduce the cost in human lives.

weather; rapid evacuation of all its people during a cyclone remains an impossibility.

The Bangladesh government has built some 200 cyclone shelters in recent years, but in 1985 there were few, if any, on Urir Char. Faced with the oncoming storm, most residents retreated to the highest spots available—the roofs of their four- or five-foot-high thatch huts—to wait and pray. Rising winds and waters soon claimed those fragile perches, drowning as many as 5,000 islanders. Some survived by clinging to debris or by riding the storm surge to the mainland or to the neighboring island of Sandwip a few miles away. A bush that refused to be uprooted saved 70-year-old Abu Qued, while his wife and six other family members were swept into the bay. Abdul Jalil, another Urir Char peasant, lost 10 of his 14-member clan. He had come from Sandwip a few years before, after weathering the disastrous 1970 cyclone there far better than his lands did. Newer and less populated, Urir Char had seemed full of promise then. Now, Jalil's sad, lined face bore no tears, his mind no thoughts of setting out for yet another landfall.

Where could he go? he wondered. More than a week after the storm had passed, he and other survivors still wandered about distractedly, some just staring, some wading the flooded paddies where bloated animal carcasses and human excrement rolled in brackish waves. Though they owned little enough before the cyclone hit, now they had only the skirt-like *lungis* and shirts they happened to be wearing. Their homes, their fields, their dreams, many of their relatives and friends, were gone. Most did not even have rudimentary shelter from sun or rain. They huddled on earthen mounds that had supported their homes and that in many areas represented the only land now above sea level. Here they waited for government helicopters to arrive and dispense the meager relief meals. A handful of *chirra* (rolled rice), a dry biscuit or two, and a gloppy lump of *gur* (crude sugar) comprised their usual daily ration. They lined up silently, stoically, never cutting ahead or begging for more, showing no impatience, only bewilderment. If you asked about the calamity, they replied without rancor or wails, saying only that it was the will of Allah.

Perhaps the cyclone was. But credit its deadliness to lack of adequate shelters, which could have prevented most if not all deaths on Urir Char, just as storm cellars in Oklahoma help minimize that state's annual tornado toll. A workable plan for evacuation also would have helped, as would the introduction of certain land reforms. The people of the chars are squatters or sharecroppers; their greatest worry apart from cyclones is that someone will take their land from them, or that a landlord will make them move.

Even after the 1985 storm, when Urir Char's remoteness hampered deliveries of emergency supplies and surviving residents were advised to leave their home for temporary relief centers nearby, almost none did. This despite Urir Char's severe shortages of food and fresh water, its near-total lack of housing or sanitation, its extensively salt-poisoned lands, the growing risk of contagion, and the complications posed by the oncoming rainy season. The people stayed because they feared their departure, no matter how brief, would only prompt others to move in permanently on their ravaged homesteads. Indeed, just days after the storm struck, new arrivals began to appear on Urir Char, seeking plots whose tenants had perished.

In hope of discouraging such disaster-bred opportunism, the government soon pledged to give or lease some char land to those who had worked it. This was good news for a fraction of the peasantry—but now more and more Bangladeshis will be tempted to squat ever sooner on newly emerging chars, long before the islets stabilize or shelters can be built. And so this new policy could actually lead to more destruction from future cyclones.

Often, in many Third World countries, people have no option but to live in areas vulnerable to nature's fury. But in the United States, some coastal developers choose to build on barrier islands and other unstable, storm-prone stretches of beachfront, regardless of the land's mobility and the world's rising sea level. When storms and erosion occur, residents and developers call for jetties, abutments, and groins—at public cost—which often aggravate rather than mitigate erosion. Damages skyrocket even in the wake of small storms, because the "improved" beach is now so much more valuable. This sort of risky development probably won't abate until our hunger for beachfront housing does.

Similarly, construction projects continue to flourish in many parts of California, a state laced with geologic faults and vulnerable to intense earthquake activity. A major San Francisco earthquake today would generate thousands of times more dollar damage than did its famous predecessor of 1906, simply because the city is now so much larger and construction costs are so much greater. Yet building keeps on booming, encouraged perhaps by confidence in our ability to produce quake-resistant structures, by our reluctance to accept the probability of major tremors, and by the conviction that the good life in San Francisco is well worth the risk of a once-in-a-century great earthquake.

We are fortunate that our country's regions of intense seismic activity are relatively few; many Latin American nations have areas at least as active but are far less generously endowed with open land. Agricultural pressures encourage utilization of limited flatland for farming, thus forcing cities and especially slum areas to expand onto steeper and more unstable terrain. And because nations of the Third World often cannot afford extensive earthquake-resistant construction, even their newest buildings don't always stand up to the restless nature of their lands. The result: A moderate quake in Nicaragua or Mexico or Chile usually causes far more deaths and damage than one of equal magnitude would in California's San Fernando Valley.

When it comes to volcanoes, this "disaster gap" between developed and developing countries widens even further. In the contiguous United States, for example, not only do eruptions occur much less often than our generally infrequent strong earthquakes, but also we inhabit active volcanic regions only sparsely, if at all. We do not have to colonize the flanks of volcanoes, as do islanders in densely populated (and densely cratered) Indonesia or the Caribbean. The eruption in 1902 of Martinique's Mont Pelée killed virtually all of the 30,000 people in the city of St. Pierre, which has never fully recovered.

Even amply proportioned mainland countries of the Third World can suffer excessively from volcanic activity. Often they are agrarian; their farmers tend to seek out volcanic soils—rich in potassium and other minerals—rather than rely on costly chemical fertilizers. By putting every volcanic shoulder and gully to the plow, however, they swell the population of high-risk areas—and add to future death tolls. The 1985 eruption of Nevado del Ruiz in Colombia set off mudflows that entombed 23,000 and left many thousands homeless.

In contrast, the eruption of Mount St. Helens five years earlier claimed only 57 lives. Not that it was a weak sister; Mount St. Helens belched rock, ash, and steam in a nine-hour eruption that released energy calculated to be the equivalent of 24 megatons. It unleashed a gigantic rockslide-avalanche more than half a cubic mile in volume; blew down 3.7 billion board feet of timber across some 250 square miles; and melted enough snow and ice to bloat the Toutle River to ten times its normal width. But its pre-eruption activity, unlike that of Nevado del Ruiz, was very closely monitored—and its surroundings were relatively unpopulated. The Colombian volcano especially hurt nearby farmers, many of whom ignored its preliminary puffs of ash and steam for several months in hope of harvesting their crops of cotton, rice, and coffee. The government's failure to order evacuations—or to take other precautions recommended by domestic and foreign geologists—also contributed to the resulting disaster. Armero, a town 30 miles from the volcano, suffered most despite its distance, because it lay along a natural drainage that channeled mudflows directly to—and through—it.

Violent as Ruiz and St. Helens were, they and even Pelée were far less destructive than some other volcanoes of history. Indonesia's Mount Tambora threw perhaps a hundred times more material skyward in 1815 than did St. Helens, blocking enough solar heat to produce the "year without a summer" of 1816. That year, killing frosts in June, July, and even August repeatedly surprised New Englanders; central Europe endured failed harvests and famine, caused by record-setting cold and wet weather. The somewhat lesser eruption of Krakatau in 1883 sent fine dusts several times around the earth, generating spectacular sunsets for months and also depressing world temperatures. As these upheavals show, climatic events such as El Niño are not the only rampages of nature to wreak global consequences.

Yet man rarely anticipates the grim aftereffects of natural disturbances, even when they are localized, even when they have occurred before. Records reveal that Nevado del Ruiz erupted in the 16th and 19th centuries, spawning mudflows remarkably similar to the one that devastated Armero in 1985. Vesuvius is another repeat offender, periodically driving people from its flanks—which are invariably repopulated, thus perpetuating disaster.

How will we cope with the next one? Today's strategy consists mainly of waiting for each catastrophe to occur, then mounting campaigns for disaster relief: Victims must be rescued from wreckage and provided with food, clothing, shelter, and medical aid; disease must be controlled, the dead buried. Certainly these are necessary and humane goals. Reaching across continents to help survivors of every natural disaster is an enormous task, encumbered with steadily rising costs, increasingly severe destruction, and the need to reach more and more victims, often in remote and impoverished areas.

Again and again Western nations—the United States in particular—have shown great generosity, on governmental levels and through relief organizations such as the Red Cross, as well as through private donations and special charity events. Live Aid—the largest rock concert ever, held simultaneously on both sides of the Atlantic in 1985—grossed more than 100 million dollars for drought victims in Africa. It was truly a noble and generous gesture—but will it achieve its stated aim of ending suffering and starvation? While the money raised can buy a lot of grain, it cannot feed millions of starving Africans for long. Developed nations must go beyond the first step—disaster relief—and help Africa forestall erosion and heal its wounded lands. Otherwise we will be treating only symptoms, not causes, and famine ultimately will return—devastating tomorrow's peasants just as it has today's.

Even the world's more traditional relief agencies are now starting to point out the inadequacy of emergency aid alone, and are emphasizing alternative measures that can greatly reduce the number and severity of natural disasters. Anders Wijkman, secretary-general of the Swedish Red Cross, has repeatedly called for such changes. The public, he writes, "must come to see disasters not simply as 'acts of God' striking helpless people, but as the results of the complex ways in which people operate within their environment. They must come to understand that charity and concern are most effective when they begin before, not after, the disaster."

Already, such advice has generated positive responses. The plight of Bangladesh—labeled "an international basket case" by Henry Kissinger just over a decade ago—prompted the U.S. government to provide not only major donations of food, supplies, and money, but also the modern storm-monitoring system currently in operation there. The Netherlands, long renowned for its success in using dikes and pumps to push back the North Sea, is now employing similar techniques to bolster some Bangladeshi chars. As part of the same land-reclamation project, the Dutch plan to build a dam between one island and the mainland to block tidal currents; embankments and cyclone shelters would protect settlers on the new land.

In addition to such technological remedies, there are now experiments with economic ones. Relief agencies such as Christian Aid and Oxfam support Bangladeshi farmers' cooperatives and other self-help groups that seek a measure of political and economic power for the peasantry. Sales of local crafts and farm products, it is hoped, will eventually raise enough money to enable peasants to erect their own storm shelters and rebuild damaged huts, rather than rely totally on their government. Progress comes slowly here, not just because the people are poor but also because they traditionally see nature's violence as too fearsome for them to combat. The real tragedy of Bangladesh is that so much of the death it repeatedly endures could be prevented through better planning and preparation. There is a need to share the knowledge and technology that only some countries now possess.

It is a need that has become all too widespread, and it is particularly urgent in countries like Mexico. In the catastrophe of 1985, Mexico City suffered especially because of the shaking of an old lake bed in response to the distant earthquake source.

In those parts of the city above the lake bed, the vibration was slow, about two seconds per swing, and buildings that happened to sway at that rate collapsed.

Such lessons of nature are complex, and the appropriate defensive actions we take will also be complex. Costly quake-resistant structures, for example, are not the only answer.

*N*umerous inexpensive precautions can be taken, but earthquake-prone areas often overlook them. Japan and California, for example, are urbanized, financially well-off, and seismically active—but until recently they coped with the everyday risk of earthquakes somewhat differently. Although both now seek expensive and complicated technological solutions in building design and earthquake-prediction methods, Japan is years ahead in adopting simple, ready-to-go measures. Measures such as strapping home water heaters and furnaces solidly in place so that quakes won't topple them, thereby not only reducing the hazard of fire but also preserving an emergency water supply. After all, the main agent of destruction in San Francisco's 1906 quake was fire, not shaking.

Other inexpensive safeguards widely used in Japan include bolting down office desks and heavy equipment to minimize injuries, and applying a film to windows so that glass shards won't rain down on people below. Vibration-sensitive switches that respond to tremors by automatically cutting off the flow of fuel to appliances powered by gas, kerosene, and oil represent another way of shrinking the risk of fire; such switches are common in Japan. For many years Japanese schools and offices have had earthquake drills and other precautionary instruction. Only since 1985

FOLLOWING PAGES: Smoldering Mount Usu, a volcano in southwestern Hokkaido, Japan, has let loose several great eruptions while looming over Toya Lake and a hot spring spa, Toyako Onsen. It spews out quantities of rock and ash, which heavy rain may transform into a swift, mud-like lahar—one

have California schools been required by law to hold regular earthquake drills and develop emergency plans, and today the state's Office of Emergency Services reports a steady increase in public awareness. The Japanese government spends about a hundred dollars per person each year on earthquake preparedness; in states at risk, the U.S. spends nowhere near that amount, though considerable support comes from the private sector.

One reason for this discrepancy, of course, is that Japan has many more severe earthquakes than the U.S. and has coped with them far longer. Other, less obvious reasons may be rooted in our pioneer past, perhaps in our dual habits of letting sleeping dogs lie—and of jumping in immediately with an indomitable, help-your-neighbor spirit whenever disaster strikes. One habit has helped create historical hardships such as the dust bowl of the 1930s; the other has helped conquer them. Our gritty sense of community continues to resurface on command: After a tornado leveled 90 percent of Barneveld, Wisconsin, in 1984, the town vowed to rebuild rather than fade away.

We usually deal capably with misfortune when we have to, but often we prefer to think that it can't or won't happen here. Call it a knock-on-wood reaction, an irrational fear that just talking about the risk of a natural upheaval can actually cause that upheaval to occur. But as we learn more about nature's violent moods, we may come to accept their inevitability. With the help of experts who study nature's rampages, we can also learn how best to prepare and protect ourselves. The knowledge already exists; sharing and implementing it could well prevent most natural hazards from becoming natural disasters.

of volcanism's most destructive aspects. Steep terrain and a lot of water enable lahars to roar downhill as fast as 60 miles an hour, sweeping along boulders, tree stumps, and other debris in terrifying displays. With its long history of quakes and eruptions, Japan ranks as a world leader in developing and implementing ways to cope with such forces. Check dams, for example, ascend Mount Usu's natural drainages crosswise like treads of a stair, and concrete walls line the gullies; they slow and direct the inevitable lahars, thus limiting damage and buying time for residents to evacuate the town.

JOEL SACKETT (FOLLOWING PAGES)

Preparing for earthquakes, schoolchildren in Fujieda, Japan, crouch beneath their desks (below, right) during a drill that teaches them how to react to minimize injury from flying objects and falling debris. Escape chutes and protective headgear of quilted cloth (below) provide a quick, safe exit from schools beset by quakes or fires. Registering some 10,000 tremors a year—mostly minor ones—Japan also promotes adult preparedness through educational advertising and mobile simulators that mimic the feel of a major temblor, so that people will recognize and respond appropriately to the real thing.

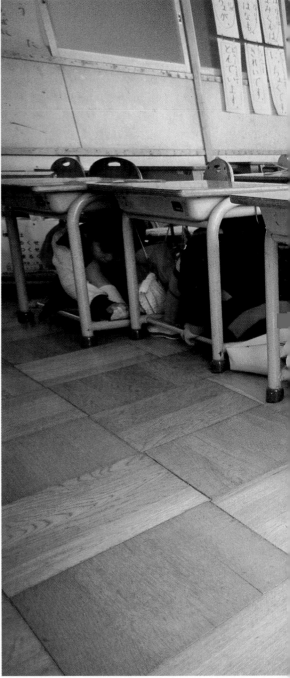

FOLLOWING PAGES: *Chaos of concrete, Mexico City's Benito Juárez Hospital collapsed in the 1985 earthquake—while the parking garage next door stood firm. Flawed design and construction added to the quake's heavy toll. As the city rebuilds, lower and more resilient structures may replace many that toppled.*

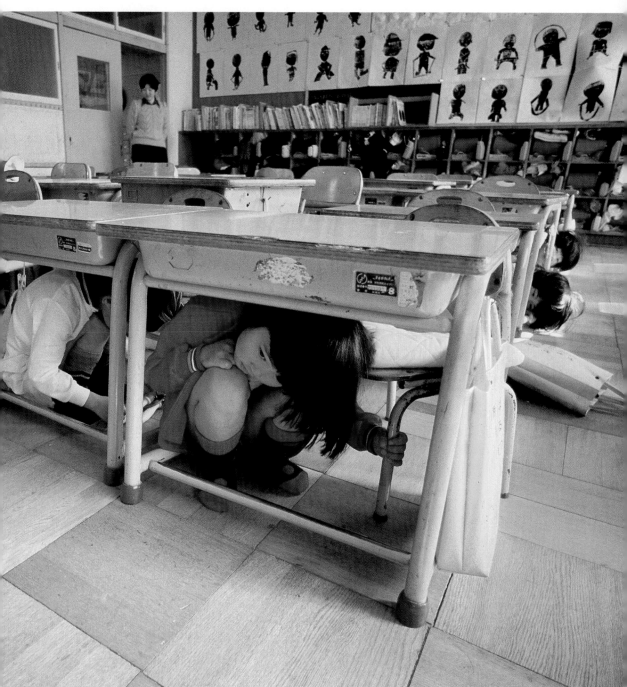

One of nature's seasonal rampages—snow—clamps a white stranglehold on Cleveland's traffic (opposite), stymies a Columbus commuter (right), and forces another Ohio motorist to abandon his stalled van for slower but more reliable transportation (below). In terms of numbers of people affected, the snowiest belt in the U.S. overlies not the Rocky Mountains but the southern tier of the Great Lakes, where major cities coincide with rising, moist air and frigid temperatures that produce some of the nation's worst snowstorms. Some towns in western New York State average 150 inches of white stuff annually—far more than Denver or Salt Lake City. For this excess, residents pay—with delays and inconveniences, with storm-related deaths, and with enormous

economic costs. Lost time from work, sharply reduced commerce, substantial cleanup expense, and frequent road repairs (prompted by use of ice-melting salts that greatly accelerate highway corrosion) all add up to an annual multibillion-dollar headache each time winter revisits the U.S.

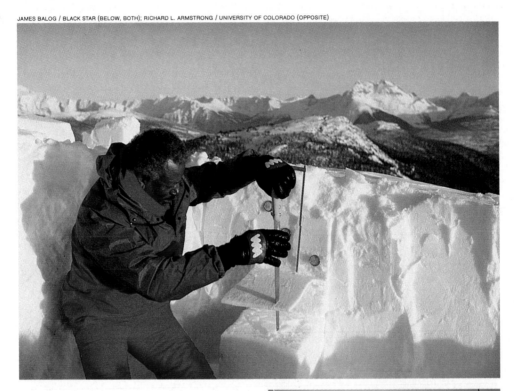

Awesome in both speed and strength, an avalanche can exceed 100 miles an hour and generate shock waves powerful enough to flatten buildings or toss trucks into the air. Artillery fire triggers a moderate slide in Colorado's San Juan Mountains (opposite) before the snowpack accumulates to killer proportions. Mountains in the western U.S. spawn some 100,000 avalanches yearly, and even experts cannot always predict them accurately. One reason: Snowfall is not uniform, but a complex laminate of many different crystal types; each layer has its own physical properties. Researcher Bill Harrison in the Cariboo Mountains of British Columbia isolates one snow slab (above) to test its shear tendency, then checks its crystal structure with a hand lens (right).

BILL NATION / PICTURE GROUP (BELOW); RAVELL CALL / PICTURE GROUP (ABOVE)

Miles beyond its usual margin, Utah's Great Salt Lake laps at the Union Pacific railbed (below) and Interstate 80 (below and left) just west of Salt Lake City. No exit drains the lake, which collects runoff from nearby mountains and inflow from rivers, but over the past several thousand years evaporation has more than offset this. Still, short-term cycles of expansion and recession occur, sometimes dramatically. After dropping to a historic low in 1963, Great Salt Lake benefited from unusually snow-heavy winters to hit a record high in June 1986—its level raised more than 20 feet and its size nearly tripled in only 23 years. In 1983 floodwaters from snowmelt raged through Salt Lake City.

Perennial victims of tropical storms, ever shifting islands at the mouths of the Ganges-Brahmaputra in Bangladesh took another beating in May 1985. A cyclone ripped into Sandwip (above), destroying a footbridge and heaving cargo boats ashore. Worst hit was nearby Urir Char, where a storm surge erased boats, crops, and homes—and drowned many of the people. A few Urir Char survivors (above, left) grieve for some of the estimated 10,000 Bangladeshis who died, far fewer than the half million killed by a similar storm in 1970. Another peasant finds solace in prayer (left). The distant concrete hut—one of only two buildings to endure on the island—serves as a relief center; by constructing more of them as storm shelters, the country could help mitigate future disasters.

Seeking any port in a storm, shrimpers from Alabama put in at Lake Charles, Louisiana, as Hurricane Danny crashes ashore in August 1985 (opposite). Labor Day weekenders at Miami Beach weather a blast from 1979's Hurricane David (above), which took more than 1,000 lives in the Dominican Republic.

FOLLOWING PAGES: Ten days after David's U.S. arrival, Frederic's 12-foot surge and 145-mph gusts made jackstraws of the boat shed at Alabama's Dauphin Island Marina. From 1979 through 1985, U.S. hurricane damage totaled 8.8 billion dollars—yet development of vulnerable coastlands continues.

Earth's Restless Face

by Ron Fisher

*"Scarcely had they reached
    the town ....
    when they felt the earth
tremble beneath them.*

*The sea boiled up
    in the harbour and
broke the ships
    which lay at anchor.
Whirlwinds of flame
    and ashes covered
the streets and squares.
    Houses came
        crashing down ....
Thirty thousand men,
women and children were
    crushed to death
        under the ruins ....*

*The terrified Candide
    stood weltering in blood
    and trembling with
fear and confusion.
    'If this is the best
        of all possible worlds,'
he said to himself,
    'what can the rest
    be like? ...'"*

—Voltaire, *Candide*

The earthquake that the fictional Candide survived was real enough, though Voltaire had his figures wrong. Actually, some 60,000 people died in the great Lisbon earthquake of 1755.

The survivors were no doubt mystified by the catastrophe that befell them. How to explain this violent shaking of the earth? They probably wondered, as did Candide, how a compassionate Creator could permit such horror. Candide never found an answer, only resignation: "... we must go and work in the garden," he finally said.

Similarly, I found questions and resignation, but few answers, when I went to Colombia in November 1985, after the eruption of Nevado del Ruiz. This volcano west of Bogotá appears on a Spanish colonial map of 1570. There it is, a flaming mountain in the central Andean cordillera. One hundred and forty years after its last major eruption, in 1845, it again came to life. On November 13, while the citizens of Armero were preparing for bed, Nevado del Ruiz coughed, sputtered, and spewed out enough hot ash to melt some of the snow and ice on its summit. A torrent of mud and water—called a lahar—swept down the precipitous slopes. In the morning, Armero, a city of 25,000, was virtually gone, buried beneath a thick blanket of ooze. From the air, it looked as if a giant load of wet concrete had been spilled down the lush and fertile valley. Green treetops and a few roofs protruded from the mud, hinting at vanished streets and roads. Highways disappeared into the muck as if into the side of a hill.

On the ground, the horror was much closer at hand. A few days after the disaster, with some companions, I drove to what was left of Armero. Even a mile away there was a sweet and sickly odor, like that of flowers left too long in a vase. We donned white surgical masks. The road ended in a slowly drying bank of mud. We got out of the car. A gasping heifer, coated with mud, lay dying at the roadside. Human bodies, turning black in the sun, lay where the flood had carried them. Cars and trucks, submerged to their windows, told of last-minute efforts to flee.

And still the birds sang; the treetops were alive with their merry chirping.

Around us was a sea of mud, where once had flourished a prosperous city. More than 20,000 people were buried here—a piteous and grotesque cemetery. In the area, the lahar destroyed 50 schools, 400 businesses, 50,000 head of cattle, 9 bridges, 110 miles of highways and local roads, 3 hydroelectric plants, 10 miles of railroad tracks, and 12,000 acres of crops.

The disaster in Colombia was unusual in that more people died than were driven from their homes, and the dead outnumbered the injured by about five to one.

"It is easier to count the living than the dead," said a ham radio operator.

"God, what have you done to us?" asked a survivor.

At Ibagué, 50 miles from Armero, where 3,000 refugees had been taken, I visited local teacher David Rocha. He took me to a hospital that had been quickly established at the local American School. Betty Wilmott, a Presbyterian nurse from Minnesota who had spent 35 years in Colombia, introduced me to some of her patients.

They were a pitiful lot—men, women, and children lying impassive in their beds, bewildered and frightened. Most, bruised from head to foot, looked as if they had been tumbled in a rock-polishing machine. It was agony for them to move. Their eyes were bright red from sulfur, grit, and tears.

One woman was within a few days of giving birth. "Her family fled when the mud came and were all killed," said Betty. "She was not able to run, got left behind, and survived."

"The patients' spirits are not too bad, considering what they've been through. Their moods and complaints seem to come in waves. They'll all get headaches or begin to cry at the same time."

As I sat in a shady spot in the courtyard of the school, a beautiful little girl approached me, grinning shyly. We tried to converse in fragments of two languages. "You live in Ibagué?" I asked her. The smile disappeared, and she looked at the ground. "No," she murmured. "Armero."

David took me to a refugee center in Ibagué for *damnificados*—people who had lost everything. Most had moved elsewhere by the time of my visit, but in a tiny room on the top floor of an abandoned office building that had been turned over to them, we found a middle-aged schoolteacher and his wife. They had been away from Armero at the time of the disaster, so had survived, but they were left with only the clothes they were wearing. She was lying on the bed and never spoke; he sat staring out of a window. Ibagué is known as a musical city, he told me. "Here the people sing. But today, no. Their heart is. . . ." He thumped his chest and turned away.

At the airport in Ibagué, a little girl on a stretcher was going to Bogotá with her father. He knelt by her side, tenderly feeding her sips of milkshake. People came by to comfort her and squeeze her hand; no one asked where her mother was.

But life went on. In the main square of a town near Armero, children laughed and played in the spill from a tanker truck filled with drinking water, even as their parents

studied lists of the dead posted on a nearby wall. Dogs slunk underfoot and looked at me with frightened eyes.

Why weren't the people of Armero warned? Surely there had been some indication that Nevado del Ruiz was reawakening. The year before, instruments had detected tremors in the mountain, and in September 1985 there were more tremors and a small eruption. A month later Armero residents were noticing mud and sulfur in the Lagunilla River, which runs through the city. In early November a Colombian geological institute said there was a 67 percent chance that an eruption would cause mudflows. Small earthquakes increased on November 10, and on the 12th the smell of sulfur was very strong. On the 13th, an emergency committee, meeting in Ibagué, recommended the evacuation of Armero. There was still time.

Why, then, were the people caught in the catastrophe that night, when torrents of mud came hurtling down the mountain at 30 miles an hour?

Local officials and Radio Armero made predisaster announcements that were meant to reassure people rather than prepare them. Thus residents didn't know what to do because they were unaware of the hazards that threatened them.

Today, local newspapers publish frequent accounts of the volcano's activity. Signs tell people where to go in case of another eruption. An early warning system will trigger an alarm at the volcano observatory as mudflows begin their descent. A communications network is now in place, and evacuation procedures are practiced.

The location and dynamics of volcanic activity involve a fairly new theory: plate tectonics. I remember the hoots of derision that greeted the concept in a freshman

geology class I took in the late '50s. The professor presented it as an example of the ridiculous, far-out theories some geologists were then expounding in an attempt to explain earth's mechanics. He got a good laugh, but today, after some 30 years of evidence has accumulated, it seems to most geologists the likeliest version of the truth.

Briefly, it describes a planet that is constantly in motion, almost a living organism. Its fiery heart beats far below. Just as hot air rises in a room and flows horizontally along the ceiling, so heat from within the earth rises to the surface and sets it simmering and sliding. The earth's outer skin is made up of about 12 large slabs called tectonic plates—from the Greek *tektōn*, meaning carpenter or builder. They may measure thousands of miles across but are

Ridge, an undersea mountain system 46,000 miles long that circles the earth like the seam of a baseball. Where plates meet, geologic chaos may trigger earthquakes and volcanic eruptions. One plate may slide beneath another in a process called subduction; or plates may grind past each other along a fault; or their collision may uplift mountain ranges, such as the Himalayas. Orange dots on the map indicate moderate and major earthquakes since 1961; red triangles represent selected active volcanoes. Many rim the vast Pacific Basin, in a volcanic zone known as the Ring of Fire.

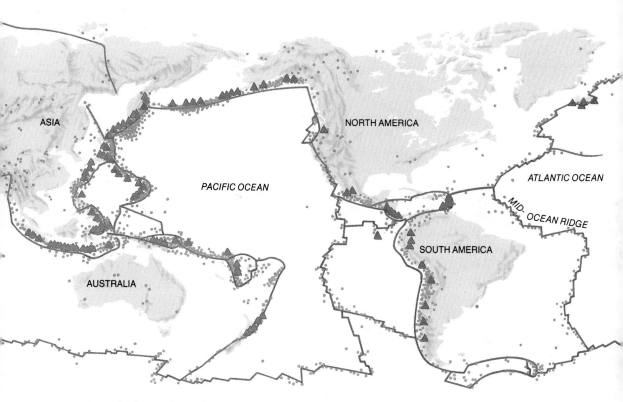

comparatively thin—about the same, in relation to the earth, as an eggshell to an egg. Atop these crustal plates, say geologists, are the continents. As the plates move, they collide with one another like gigantic bumper cars. Along their margins occur the major geologic events—eruptions and earthquakes—that can so devastatingly affect life on earth.

Magma is continuously being extruded along the Mid-Ocean Ridge, an undersea mountain system 46,000 miles long. As plates move away from each other at the ridge, new material is added to their edges in a process called seafloor spreading. Thus the ocean floor near the ridge is among the youngest material on earth—and nowhere is it more than 200 million years old.

Where two plates collide, subduction

usually occurs: One plate carrying seafloor may descend beneath another plate into the interior of the earth, forming an ocean trench and triggering deep earthquakes. As the slab descends, magma may move up fractures in the overlying plate and form a chain of volcanoes. The Andes are such a chain. Or a collision between plates may cause an upthrusting of mountains. A good example of this is the Indian subcontinent, which is plowing into Eurasia and causing the Himalayas to rise. This collision triggers powerful and often destructive earthquakes in the area.

Most quakes are born of strike-slip faulting, a phenomenon caused by plates grinding past one another and forming huge rips, or faults, on their adjacent edges. These zones can become locked and find release dramatically, with a big lurch. Part of California moved north as much as 20 feet along the San Andreas Fault during the great San Francisco quake of 1906.

Some volcanoes arise mysteriously through the middle of a plate. Somehow magma accumulates in a hot spot beneath the plate, then melts or forces its way to the surface; as the plate moves above it, the hot spot stays behind, building a chain of volcanoes. The Hawaiian Islands are emerging from such a hot spot. Eroded and submerged islands in the chain stretch north almost to Siberia as the Emperor Seamounts, and another Hawaiian island, still a-building, lies some 3,000 feet below the surface of the ocean south of the island of Hawaii. Yellowstone's geysers and mud pots sit atop another hot spot. So does Iceland—where, incidentally, the largest lava flow in recorded history erupted in 1783.

Thus, according to plate tectonic theory, earthquakes and eruptions occur largely at plate boundaries, where cracks appear in earth's thin shell. A global map showing historic seismic events follows almost exactly the outlines of the plates.

The ancients had a less precise understanding of earth's mechanics. Plato thought there were underground channels through which the four elements—earth, wind, fire, and air—swirled into caverns, out of which volcanoes arose. In the Middle Ages, when common knowledge placed hell in the center of the earth, volcanoes were thought to be the entrances to that dark world; the sounds they made were the howls and groans of the damned. And sulfur dioxide, a common volcanic gas with the pungent odor of burning sulfur, may have been the biblical brimstone.

Some of earth's most cataclysmic events have been volcanic eruptions. When Mount Mazama in what is now called the Cascade Range erupted 7,000 years ago, its ash fell as far away as Alberta and British Columbia and covered an area of 5,000 square miles to a depth of six inches. Avalanches of ash and pumice raced nearly 40 miles. The huge crater left by the eruption filled to become Oregon's Crater Lake.

The first eruption to be described carefully was that of Mount Vesuvius in A.D. 79. Pliny the Elder—who had written, "There can be no doubt that conflagrations are a punishment inflicted upon us for our luxury"—died then, and his nephew, Pliny the Younger, wrote an account of his death and the catastrophe that caused it.

A philosopher of natural history, Pliny the Elder was living at Misenum, across the Bay of Naples from Vesuvius, when the mountain erupted. On the afternoon of August 24, his sister hurried into his room and told him that a large cloud had formed above Vesuvius. Across the bay in Pompeii, volcanic bombs came hurtling out of the sky. Thousands fled the darkened city; Pliny ordered a ship to take him there, but was unable to land because of falling pumice. He sailed farther down the coast to Stabiae, where he feared an old friend might be in danger. There he watched "broad sheets of fire and leaping flames" coursing down Vesuvius. Pliny insisted on having a bath and going to bed—partly to reassure his host there was no danger—but he was awakened in the morning to find a household in alarm. The courtyard was full of volcanic debris, and earthquakes rocked the villa. Pliny and his friend held pillows over their heads and hurried toward Pliny's ship. The sea was too rough to launch it. Pliny lay down to catch his breath, but was soon roused and urged to flee as flaming clouds of gas approached. Supported by two slaves, the elderly philosopher staggered a few steps, then fell dead.

It may have been a heart attack that killed Pliny, or it may have been the lethal gases issuing from Vesuvius. Almost 2,000 people died in Pompeii, largely from suffocation in a deadly cloud of ash. Up the coast, a glowing cloud of hot ash and pumice swept over Herculaneum, killing hundreds who had sought refuge along the waterfront. Later, five ash avalanches buried the city up to a depth of 60 feet or more.

One of the most cataclysmic eruptions in history came in 1883, when a volcano on the Indonesian island of Krakatau exploded. It had been sputtering for months, but in late August there came a series of explosions, the largest on the 27th. If Krakatau had exploded in Kansas, people on both coasts would have known, for the sound of it was heard 3,000 miles away; it may have been the loudest sound ever heard on our planet. For months, the world was treated to spectacular, fiery sunsets as tons of ash high in the atmosphere circled the globe.

*L*ava from a volcanic eruption is virtually unstoppable and overwhelms everything in its path. Rarely have humans successfully altered the course of a lava flow. When the 1973 eruption on the island of Heimaey, off the south coast of Iceland, threatened to close the harbor, the determined islanders resolved to fight back. Attaching hoses to their town's water supply, they directed streams of cold water onto the leading edge of the advancing lava. Encouraged by the results, they brought a pump ship into the harbor, borrowed large pumps from the U.S. Navy, and began pouring millions of gallons of seawater onto the lava. Using bulldozers (with fearless drivers), they also laid a network of 19 miles of sprinkler pipes on the surface of the hot lava. Though much of their town was eventually destroyed or damaged, the Icelanders managed to save their harbor. Scientists estimated that the lava cooled and solidified 50 to 100 times faster than it would have on its own. Ten years later, the Italians used both explosives and earthen

barriers to divert major flows during an eruption of Mount Etna.

By and large, the United States has been spared the fury of volcanoes, but in May 1980 Mount St. Helens in Washington State roared to life. In March scientists had recorded moderate earthquakes in the area around Mount St. Helens, and the mountain had emitted a plume of ash 7,000 feet high. In April an enormous bulge on the north face began to move as much as five feet a day. On May 18 a quake loosened it and sent a massive rockslide-avalanche down the mountain. Hot gases carried debris outward at high velocities, flattening 250 square miles of forest. Clouds of ash and pulverized rock shot into the sky. Gray floodwaters poured down river valleys. About 60 people were dead or missing after the eruption, and bridges, roads, crops, and homes were destroyed.

Had Mount St. Helens been nearer a heavily populated area, instead of in relative wilderness, loss of life and property would have been much greater. And in many countries of the world, that would have been the case—for the slopes of volcanoes have fertile soils and are popular places of habitation, in spite of the dangers. These include not only lava flows but also pyroclastic flows, the turbulent mixtures of gases and rocks that can sweep across the ground at a hundred miles an hour; tephra, the volcanic bombs and ash that fall from the sky; mudflows, such as the one that buried Armero; forest fires; debris avalanches and landslides; and even lightning. As Mount St. Helens erupted, climbers miles away on another mountain felt electric charges in their ice axes.

But volcanoes bring benefits as well as destruction. It may even be that without them earth might never have become a habitable planet. Some scientists say that both the water of the oceans and the gases of the early atmosphere were derived from the cooling of subsurface magma and reached the surface of the planet through hot springs and volcanoes. Volcanism has helped build the continents and nearly all oceanic islands. Magma is a potentially useful source of geothermal energy, and

Subduction ignites deep fires that can snuff out cities without warning. Here the Nazca plate, on the left, slides beneath the continental crust of the American plate. As it moves, it creates the offshore Peru-Chile Trench, one of several deep ocean trenches that border the Ring of Fire. Worldwide,

ocean floor descends into subduction zones at a rate that would devour the entire surface of the earth every 160 million years. Friction from a plate's descent creates heat that seeks release upward. Earthquakes may result, or magma may reach the surface as erupting lava. The long chain of the Andes rose because

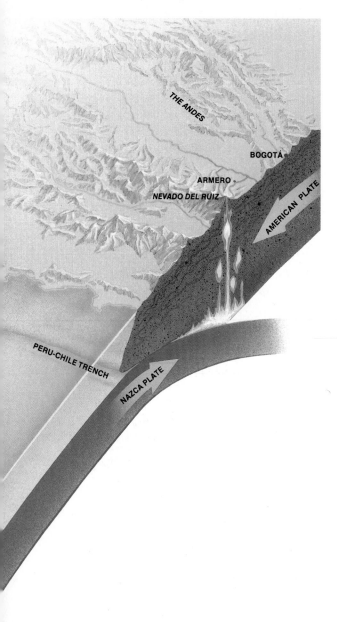

THE ANDES

BOGOTÁ

ARMERO

NEVADO DEL RUIZ

AMERICAN PLATE

PERU-CHILE TRENCH

NAZCA PLATE

many volcanic areas make wonderfully scenic parks and recreation areas.

Periodic applications of volcanic ash can add greatly to the fertility of soil. The slopes above Armero, for instance, were thick with coffee plantations, and farmers still crowd the slopes of Vesuvius. In 1906 the *New York Times*, reporting renewed volcanic activity from Vesuvius, said: "Only this is sure. The sides and neighborhoods of Vesuvius will be inhabited until the very last habitability, and, even if the great devastation comes, people will go creeping back afterward. . . ."

So actually two things are certain: Volcanoes will continue to erupt, and people will continue to live near them. It thus becomes a matter of forecasting their behavior, not an easy task. Scientists use an arsenal of equipment to help them try to anticipate eruptions. Sensitive seismometers detect even minute earthquakes, an indication that a mountain may be coming to life. Tiltmeters and laser beams detect ground movements and bulges. Chemists analyze a volcano's seepage of gases to record changes—more or less sulfur, more or less chlorine, increases in mercury or radon—that can mean magma is approaching the surface.

"There are really two ways to forecast an eruption," Dr. Robert Decker, a geophysicist with the U.S. Geological Survey in Menlo Park, California, told me. "One is statistical, long-range forecasting. You study a mountain's historic eruptions and its prehistoric geologic record to see if it has any habits—or *lack* of habits—that might tell you what it's likely to do in the future.

"Or you physically monitor a volcano. Monitoring is much more expensive. You need 10 to 15 people, maybe 25 seismographic stations. There are only two or

of the crumpling of the American plate's western edge—and still rises. On November 13, 1985, long-dormant Nevado del Ruiz in Colombia awoke once again in an eruption that destroyed Armero, a city of 25,000. Late in 1986, increased seismic activity and volume of gases warned of surging magma.

three volcanoes in the U.S. that rate that kind of attention. But you can put a couple of seismometers on a volcano and transmit their signals by remote control to an observatory. That way, one observatory can at least keep a figurative ear to the ground on many volcanoes. That's what we're doing now in the Cascade Range.

"Our major problem with monitoring is that we can detect magma rising from deeper levels, but we can't tell if it will reach the surface."

How about actually controlling a lava flow or an eruption, or even disarming a volcano that seems about to erupt? "Certainly there's a technical potential for controlling where lava flows go, but if people start diverting them, and they end up on someone else's property, who's liable? Society hasn't worked that out yet.

"The solution to volcano forecasting involves a combination of science, politics, law, and common sense. What we scientists would like, in an ideal world, would be to make forecasting probabilistic—that is, we'd like to be able to say, 'There's a 60 percent chance that this mountain is going to erupt within a certain time frame.' Kind of like weather forecasting. Then let government officials make the decisions that affect society. No scientist wants to be put in a position of saying 'evacuate' or 'don't evacuate.' It affects your scientific objectivity. By the same token, trying to release some of the stored-up energy in a volcano—with a controlled nuclear explosion, for instance—seems risky. The solution might be worse than the problem. I think acts of God should be left to God."

Many of the tools scientists use for predicting the behavior of volcanoes also are used for studying their belligerent cousins, the earthquakes.

It's been said that earthquakes are where geology meets the public, for earthquakes, like eruptions, are disasters only when people are involved. When the earth moves, we move with it, but our bridges, buildings, and railroad tracks sometimes don't survive the trip. An earthquake that harms no one is merely the earth rearranging its face, something it does constantly. Seismometers detect thousands of minute earthquakes each year. In California alone, the yearly average is almost 15,000; the vast majority are too small for us to feel.

In the 1930s and '40s, Charles F. Richter and Beno Gutenberg of the California Institute of Technology developed the best-known system for measuring earthquakes. The scale is logarithmic—so in a quake of magnitude 5 the seismic waves measured by a seismograph are 10 times the size of those in a quake of 4; but the energy released is about 30 times as great. Quakes of less than 2 are seldom felt by people.

Quakes often occur around the Pacific Basin, along the same crustal boundaries as many volcanoes. As plates collide, one usually bends first, then eventually breaks. The sudden movement releases energy vibrations—seismic waves—that radiate out from the source of the quake like ripples in a pond. They set the entire planet vibrating like a struck bell. Some quakes are born deep within the earth, but most are of shallow origin. Those that occur along the San Andreas Fault begin less than ten miles beneath the surface.

The largest earthquakes do not necessarily do the most damage. A lot depends on surface and subsurface geologic conditions, the depth of the source, the distance from the epicenter, population density, and the design and sturdiness of the works of man. The 1964 Good Friday earthquake in Alaska was stronger, on the Richter scale, than the San Francisco quake of 1906, but because it occurred in the sparsely populated north, damage and loss of life were much less. Even so, its effects were felt over 700,000 square miles of Alaska and Canada.

Two of history's most devastating quakes occurred far from crustal boundaries in the vast interior of China. Some 830,000 people perished there in a monster quake in 1556, and about 240,000 in 1976.

German naturalist Alexander von Humboldt experienced a tremor in November 1799 in Venezuela. "When a shock is felt, when the earth is shaken on its old foundations, which we had deemed stable, one instant is sufficient to destroy long illusions. It is like awakening from a dream; but a painful awakening. We feel that we have been deceived by the apparent calm of nature; we become attentive to the least noise; we mistrust for the first time a soil on which we had so long placed our feet with confidence."

Von Humboldt favored a theory that attributed earthquakes to an abnormal absence of thunderstorms, which led to "an accumulation of electricity in the interior of the Earth." He visited Caracas after the city had been leveled by a quake in 1812. The devastation there was terrible, he wrote. "Mothers were seen bearing in their arms their children, whom they hoped to recall to life."

In the United States, quakes generally have not been so devastating, though a series of powerful ones struck near New Madrid, Missouri, in 1811 and 1812, and strong aftershocks continued for several months. Shaking was felt over much of the eastern U.S. In Kentucky, before one of the shocks, John James Audubon's horse suddenly stopped, groaned, spread its legs, and refused to budge. "At that instant," wrote Audubon, "all the shrubs and trees began to move from their very roots, the ground rose and fell in successive furrows, like the ruffled waters of a lake." People felt the quake as far away as New York City. Nearer New Madrid, fissures opened in the

ground, sections of land sank, and the courses of rivers and streams were changed. Land subsided in western Tennessee, and the depression filled with creek water to become Reelfoot Lake. Thousands of trees fell, perhaps as many as 150,000 acres of them. Riverbanks tumbled into the Mississippi, and for a while, locals claimed, the mighty river reversed its course. Modern seismologists agree that the riverbed may have risen in one or two places on February 7, 1812, stopping, temporarily at least, the Father of Waters in his tracks.

The most damaging quake in U.S. history hit San Francisco on April 18, 1906. Scientists estimate that it would have measured 8.3 on the Richter scale. It ruptured gas mains, igniting an inferno that burned four square miles of the city. Citizens crossed the bay and watched helplessly from Berkeley and Oakland. As many as 2,000 people may have perished.

On August 17, 1959, twenty-eight vacationers were killed by landslides caused by an earthquake near Yellowstone National Park. It took Old Faithful several months to get back on schedule. In the last three months of 1985, instruments recorded more than 300 quakes in the town of West Yellowstone. Only 12 measured above 4, and they did little damage, except to the nerves of the residents.

*U*nimaginably worse was the cataclysm that struck Mexico City on September 19, 1985, barely two months before Nevado del Ruiz erupted in Colombia. The city was mostly up and getting ready for work at 7:18 a.m., when the first tremor hit. Some 220 miles to the west, the Cocos plate had snapped as it edged beneath the American plate. The resulting lurch sent shock waves racing toward Mexico City at nearly 15,000 miles an hour. Seismographs recorded them at 8.1 on the Richter scale. The heart of Mexico City, built atop an old, unstable lake bed, received a series of hammerblows that toppled buildings, crushed small structures beneath towering neighbors, severed electric, gas, and telephone lines, and buried thousands of people. Some estimates say 30,000 died.

A few weeks after the quake, I stood across the street from the Regis, once a comfortable tourist hotel where I had stayed during a vacation five years before. Now it was a brown heap of dusty rubble being hosed down by grim workmen. A nearby park, where I had sat to watch the people go by, was filled with the tattered tents of the homeless. Thousands had seen their homes destroyed and had no place to go in a city chronically short of housing.

At a giant medical center, the dozen or so buildings were all abandoned and awaiting the wrecker's ball. An old accordionist sat in the autumn drizzle and entertained passersby. The sidewalks they trod were cracked and twisted.

Old colonial buildings survived the quake with little or no damage. The Metropolitan Cathedral, built with Aztec stones in 1525, was as solid as then, and the National Palace, constructed in the 1700s, looked virtually intact. But I also saw new high-rise apartment buildings that were deserted, their windows jagged with shattered glass, their corners crumbling.

"It could have been worse," a resident told me. "Mexico City is one of the world's largest cities, with some 16 million people, and though thousands of buildings were wrecked, hundreds of thousands weren't."

Structural engineers study the Mexico City quake and others as well to learn more about factors important to the design of future buildings. They have found, for instance, that a building can resonate with the frequency of the ground waves, like a child on a swing being pushed higher and higher; floors and walls will crack more and more with each swing until the structure finally collapses. One arm of an L-shaped building will sway more than the other, causing a fracture where they are joined. Similarly, a high-rise tower emerging from a lower structure will rupture at the seam. Tall buildings will sway at the top as much as five times more than at ground level. And tall buildings too close together may collide as they swing and literally pound each other to pieces.

Downtown Mexico City may look very different in the future. There will be more space between buildings, and many areas where buildings collapsed will remain open. Engineers and scientists are working together to design structures that combine rigidity and strength to withstand ground motion better. Buildings over four stories that are deemed unsafe will be razed or will lose their upper floors to reduce the natural period of vibration. Some buildings will have preventive improvements such as shear walls, which stiffen buildings and thus change their period of vibration. Construction firms will be required to follow new codes that take into account the variety of soils underlying the city.

It would be hard to imagine two places more different than Mexico City and Parkfield, California, but they are both brushed by powerful geologic forces. Parkfield, a hamlet midway between Los Angeles and San Francisco, sits an easy stone's throw from the San Andreas Fault, along the boundary of the American and Pacific plates. The west side of the fault is creeping north, except for a 15-mile-long stretch near Parkfield, where the fault combines smooth slip and partial sticking. Each passing year adds more stress and will continue to do so until there is a sudden lurch. Such abrupt slippages—which produce earthquakes—have occurred in the Parkfield area on an average of every 22 years since 1857. The U.S. Geological Survey (USGS) has predicted another one for 1988, plus or minus a few years, so scientists have flocked to Parkfield to have their instruments in place when the quake comes.

"If you put a silver dollar under the West Coast, we'd detect it with the Parkfield instruments," a USGS scientist joked. "And if anybody in Parkfield sneezes, we've got 'em covered." Creepmeters measure relative movement by means of wires strung between points on opposite sides of the fault. Dilatometers in wells hundreds of feet deep measure changes in pressure on fluid-filled metallic containers.

"Parkfield is really wired," said Duane Hamann, the only teacher in Parkfield's one-room elementary school.

I accompanied Duane one evening to the top of Car Hill, where there was a small shed with windows on all four sides. Inside was a laser. The size of a small cannon, it looked like an old-fashioned ray gun from comic books. Every other night, under a contract with the USGS and the University of Colorado, Duane spends three or four hours on top of Car Hill, firing the laser at 16 or so distant targets on both sides of the fault. The beams are reflected back by mirrors. Their transit time can be measured, and thus the distance from light source to mirror computed precisely.

We fired up the laser and aimed it at a distant mirror. A flickering red reflection showed we had hit the mark. A computer calculated the transit time and converted the reading to millimeters, and Duane charted the results. He showed me one of the graphs, a jagged line trending downward. "In one spot the west side of the fault is moving north at about an inch and a half a year," he told me. "That's about the rate fingernails grow."

Technician Tom Burdette took me to a seismic sensor buried on another hillside. Standing directly over it, I wiggled my toes and watched, astonished, as the needle on Tom's gauge leaped upward. I pulled a blade of grass and touched it lightly against the ground. The needle quivered.

Donalee Thomason's house sits half a mile from the fault just at the north edge of Parkfield. Taped to the wall by the telephone is a list of things to do in the event of an earthquake: 1) Set breakable things on floor; 2) Set TV on floor; 3) Turn off pilot light gas; 4) Turn off electricity.

"I've seen seismic waves cross the valley," Donalee told me. "They're like ocean waves, and they pass like shadows right down the valley. You hear the leaves rustling in the trees."

Every nook, cranny, shelf, and mantel in Donalee's living room held small ceramic figures, hundreds of them. Expensive Hummel figurines had their own cabinet. It seemed a risky hobby for someone living nearly atop the San Andreas Fault.

Donalee remembers two major earthquakes in Parkfield, one in 1934 and the other in 1966. "I was not quite ten in 1934, and we were having our school's year-end program in the old Parkfield Community Hall. My father, who was in charge of props, had brought an old white window frame and hung it from the ceiling so its bottom rested on the stage. Each child would come and stand just behind it, facing the audience, and give a recitation. I was backstage with the other children, waiting to go on, when the quake hit. It seemed like the building was turning upside down. Adults were screaming and trying to run, which is the worst thing you can do in an earthquake. The grown-ups decided we should go on with the program, even though we were having a lot of aftershocks. One little girl was speaking her piece when another severe aftershock hit. She jumped forward, right through the window frame, down off the stage, and into the audience. When the shock ended, she hopped back on the stage, through the frame, turned around, and never missed a word!

"In 1966 I was home here when I felt the ground move. I got some bath towels and wrapped my Hummel figures in them and put them in a box on the porch. Later, between eight and nine o'clock that night, I was standing in the open door, facing inside, when the real quake struck. The first thing I heard was like a big suction, then a hissing as the shock wave hit the house. It was like a rush of hot air. I learned then, never stand in an open door of a wood-frame house during an earthquake! The door swung shut and hit me, knocked me down on one knee. I looked up and the walls were buckling. Then the doors of that china cupboard burst open and all the dishes flew right out. They seemed to hang in midair, then crashed to the floor. Then the lights went out. There was a terrible noise behind me as our big upright freezer, with maybe 400 pounds of meat in it, fell onto its face on the back porch."

All Californians along the San Andreas Fault—not just the residents of Parkfield—have reason to worry. A series of tremors, some registering 6 or more, shook central California in July 1986. Scientists predict that there is a 50-50 chance of a quake of magnitude 8 or greater occurring on the southern section of the fault within the next 30 years. It could kill between 3,000 and 14,000 people, they say. Studies have identified unsafe building types, but little money has been appropriated for making them safe. There is one exception: The California legislature spent 62 million dollars to refurbish and strengthen its own work space, the State Capitol.

Earthquake prediction is a young science. "It was just 20 years ago—in 1965—that the first nationally sponsored proposal for earthquake prediction was written," says Dr. Robert E. Wallace, chief scientist in the USGS's Office of Earthquakes, Volcanoes, and Engineering. "Through the '70s, there was debate: Would prediction do more harm than good? By causing panic, for instance, or by stopping construction or causing insurance problems. Several studies concluded that prediction could greatly reduce casualties, and prediction was included as a goal in the National Earthquake Hazard Reduction Act of 1977. Then in 1985 the USGS issued its first formal prediction: that there would be a quake in the Parkfield area around 1988. So it took 20 years to get from proposal to prediction."

How about 20 years from now? I asked him. Where will we be?

"It's going to be a long, difficult job," he said. "I like to tell people, 'When you can cure all forms of cancer, we'll be able to predict earthquakes.' Because quakes are as complex as cancer—in some ways, maybe more complex. There are so many kinds, so many situations, so many variables. But I'm optimistic because of this: A big earthquake involves the movement of thousands of cubic miles of the earth's crust. You can't have something that big developing and not be able to see some signals. The crust of the earth has to bend before it breaks, and we're trying now to detect and measure that bending."

Among the worst hazards associated with earthquakes, and triggered by them, are tsunami. They were once called "tidal waves"—a misnomer, for they have nothing to do with tides. Their current name is Japanese for "great harbor wave," because they disturb even the quiet waters of harbors protected from wind waves. Scientists define tsunami as seismic sea waves most commonly generated by earthquakes near oceanic trenches. They may measure a hundred miles from crest to crest, yet be only a few feet high in the deep parts of the ocean. Ships at sea can't detect them, nor can they be seen from the air. Their speed depends on the depth of the water, so in the open ocean they travel up to 600 miles an hour. They represent the movement of the entire vertical section of ocean they pass through, and they can travel enormous distances without losing their energy.

It's only when they shoal—in the shallow water surrounding an island, for instance—that tsunami become a threat. Approaching an island or shallow coast, they slow and climb, sometimes reaching a hundred feet. They are often merely a continuous but rapid rising of the water—water that keeps coming and coming and coming. Tsunami have bent railroad tracks and moved locomotives, deposited large boats miles inland, stacked automobiles three deep or wrapped them around trees, washed out concrete seawalls 20 inches thick, and scattered four-ton blocks of concrete hundreds of feet. When such a wave finally reaches its peak and washes back out to sea, the rushing undertow can cause even worse damage.

Tsunami are rare in the Atlantic Ocean, though there was a brutal exception. The Lisbon earthquake that so terrified Candide dealt a double blow to the inhabitants. As buildings collapsed, fires broke out and raged into a holocaust. Residents fled for their lives to the waterfront, where they thought they would find safety. But suddenly the harbor emptied, bottoming craft and stranding fish a mile out. Then the wave came. Survivors said it was 50 feet high when it broke over Lisbon's waterfront, drowning thousands as it swept half a mile inland.

When Krakatau exploded in 1883, the eruption itself caused no casualties, for the island was uninhabited. But the resulting tsunami, a hundred feet high, crashed into the coasts of Java and Sumatra, killing more than 36,000 people. It produced waves that traveled two or three times around the globe.

A tsunami that struck Hawaii in 1946 was that state's worst-ever natural disaster. It killed 159 people and did some 25 million dollars' worth of damage. A tsunami born of an earthquake off Chile in 1960 was the most destructive in recent history: More than two thousand people died in Chile itself and in Hawaii, the Philippines, and Japan. The huge Alaska earthquake of 1964 triggered a tsunami that damaged property and claimed lives as far away as Washington, Oregon, and California.

*T*he Hawaii tsunami of 1946 was the last to take the islands by surprise. By 1948 the National Oceanic and Atmospheric Administration (NOAA) had inaugurated the Pacific Tsunami Warning System, with centers, today, in Honolulu and in Palmer, Alaska. Connected to seismometers (to detect earthquakes) and to tide gauges (to detect tsunami waves), the centers keep watch round the clock. They can provide warnings to designated emergency and relief organizations in 18 Pacific coastal and island nations and territories.

But, according to Dr. Eddie Bernard, as much as an hour can elapse between the time a tsunami is detected and the time the warning reaches the appropriate authority in some countries. And that worries him.

At NOAA's Pacific Marine Environmental Laboratory in Seattle, which he directs, Dr. Bernard told me: "Millions of people live and work in areas of the Pacific Basin that are subject to tsunami inundation. And since the early 1850s more than 70,000 have been killed by them. Because we rely on voice and teletype communication systems, some of the developing countries,

with either minimal or no regional warning systems, can't be alerted quickly enough to the danger of tsunami originating near their shores.

"So now we're working on project THRUST—Tsunami Hazard Reduction Using Satellite Technology. We're examining existing technology to see if an early warning system can be designed to get the word to developing countries more quickly. Right now, we're trying to design, assemble, test, install, and evaluate such a system in Chile." That system is now in place, and testing is under way.

From sensors on land and in the sea, real-time data will be sent to a stationary satellite overhead. If the sensors detect an earthquake large enough to generate a tsunami, in minutes data will be sent automatically to Chile. The new system, if successful, could eventually be applied throughout the Pacific.

In the cluttered labs in the basement of the NOAA building, the sensors are designed, tested, and maintained. One had been taken apart. It was a two-foot-long metal cylinder, full of batteries and circuit boards. Sticking out of one end was a tiny sensor—a barometer that measures not air pressure but the pressure of water.

"It can tell when a lot of water passes over it," said Dr. Bernard.

"There's still a good deal of work to be done on tsunami," he told me. "I think there's a perception that we know a lot more than we do. Society is making decisions—on evacuation zones and building codes and insurance rates—that are based on pretty scanty data.

"For instance, in the late '70s two numerical models were constructed. Both assumed there would be a tsunami that originated around Kodiak Island, and both

Earthquakes, the seismic shudders of our planet's skin, often occur where plates do battle. Carrying Pacific seafloor, the Cocos plate descends beneath the lighter American plate. In September 1985 a sudden fracturing of the Cocos plate, some 12 miles below the surface, sent shock waves racing across

assessed the potential damage to the West Coast. But there was a difference of a factor of four in the expected amplitude of the wave. That is, one said the wave would be four times bigger than the other. That's a pretty big spread. And if you live in San Francisco, you want to know, is this wave going to be four feet or sixteen feet high.

"So it doesn't make any sense to invest a lot of money in these numerical models until we collect appropriate data to resolve the differences. In the next decades, the data will come from our newest instruments and also from seismologists, who can now tell us pretty accurately where to expect tsunami to form."

The day I left Seattle was clear and bright, and, as I drove to the airport, there suddenly loomed off to my left the cold white mass of Mount Rainier. No doubt, when news of eruptions hits the front pages, the citizens of Seattle and Tacoma cast a speculative eye on this volcano, for it is by no means dead. Located in the same Cascade Range as Mount St. Helens, it has erupted before and will again—and all the drainages from Rainier run to the Puget Sound area. During the last 10,000 years, geologists say, there have been at least 55 mudflows from Rainier. The largest, the Osceola, some 5,000 years ago, covered an area of more than 110 square miles in the Puget Sound lowland, an area where thousands of people live today. Rainier's last recorded eruption was barely a hundred years ago, in 1882.

Still, there is little the people of Puget Sound can do but go about their business. Like Candide, we must tend our gardens, but we would do well to remember that the earth we till, and the planet we call home, can turn in an instant from beneficent provider to raging menace.

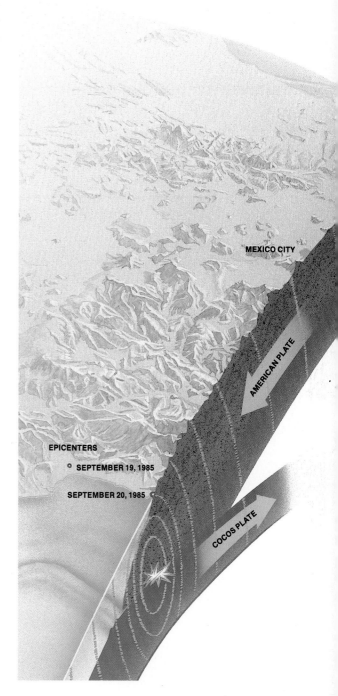

Mexico. As many as 30,000 people may have perished when tremors convulsed parts of Mexico City. Four crustal plates interact in the area of the Mexican and Colombian disasters. Their movements caused the 1976 quake in Guatemala that killed 23,000 and the 1982 eruption of Mexico's El Chichón.

FOLLOWING PAGES: Terrified women flee with their belongings as pavements gape and fires break out in Fukui, Japan, during the great earthquake of June 28, 1948. There to record the city's amazing recovery from the war, Life *photographer Carl Mydans instead captured on film its second destruction in three years.*

Ridges rise where plates collide: The San Andreas Fault, with the Pacific plate on the right and the American plate on the left, wrinkles the Carrizo Plain a hundred miles north of Los Angeles. As the plates grind past each other here, friction binds their edges. Periodic breaks in the rock shift the colossal slabs, sending shock waves radiating outward. Scientists have turned the fault— actually a complex system of faults—into a gigantic geophysical laboratory. From Mexico nearly to Oregon, seismometers detect tiny earth movements; lasers and creepmeters—whose wires stretch across the

NATIONAL GEOGRAPHIC PHOTOGRAPHER JAMES L. STANFIELD

fault—measure slippage in fractions of
millimeters; fluid-filled metallic containers
deep in wells contract under increasing stress.
Many experts warn of another major quake
along the San Andreas Fault—perhaps
equaling the 1906 jolt that leveled San
Francisco—within the next 30 years.

In the path of potential disaster, Interstate 280 curls back on itself at Daly City, barely two miles from the San Andreas Fault. A relatively moderate quake near Los Angeles in 1971 destroyed a similar configuration (below), killed 64 people, and caused half a billion dollars' worth of damage.

FOLLOWING PAGES: With many bay-side districts on shaky landfill, San Francisco may face a repeat of its 1906 catastrophe. Engineers believe quake-resistant structures such as the Transamerica Pyramid (foreground), built since the introduction of stricter codes, will withstand severe tremors.

Rocked beyond a stable limit, apartment buildings lie toppled on their backs in Mexico City. Registering 8.1 on the Richter scale, the quake that hit on September 19, 1985, damaged or destroyed an estimated 7,000 of the city's one million structures. Why did some collapse while their similar neighbors remained standing? Engineers cite a number of factors: the frequency of a building's natural vibrations in relation to the frequency of the ground waves; the building's shape and its orientation to the motion of the earth; the solidity of its foundation and substrata; the material used and the presence or absence of reinforcements; and the quality of construction. The school building at right fell in ruins before students arrived; a soldier guards against looting.

Witnesses to tragedy, rescue workers swarm over the pancaked layers of Benito Juárez Hospital. Their round-the-clock efforts revealed few survivors amid the rubble. The earthquake struck the Mexico City hospital at the worst possible time—at 7:18 a.m., when one staff was coming on duty and another going off. Nearly a thousand patients, doctors, and nurses perished in this single structure. The quake began 220 miles west of Mexico City when, 40 miles offshore, the compressed Cocos plate snapped as it edged beneath the American plate on which Mexico rides. The resulting seismic waves, traveling at almost 15,000 miles an hour, reached Mexico City in just over a minute. A magnitude-7.6 aftershock jolted the city the next day. Built up since Aztec times atop the spongy clay of a shrunken lake now largely drained and filled with silt, the city's center proved especially vulnerable. "It was like shaking a plate of Jell-O," said one geologist. "There would have been less damage if the city had been on solid rock." In addition, the low-frequency waves that rocked the area corresponded to the natural harmonics of many high-rise buildings, causing them to slowly shake themselves apart. Near the epicenter—the surface point directly above the initial fracture—the earthquake twisted coastal railroad tracks at a fertilizer plant (left); soon afterward a tsunami, a seismic sea wave resulting from the quake, washed over them and draped them with seaweed.

Fury from the sea engulfs Hilo on the island of Hawaii on April 1, 1946. In this historic photograph, a rising wall of water sweeps inland toward people fleeing down Ponahawai Street. At the harbor (below), an unidentified man on Pier I watches helplessly as the wave—and certain death—approach. He was never seen again. Tsunami—the dread oceanic surges once erroneously called tidal waves—arise from earthquakes, eruptions, or submarine landslides. They may travel thousands of miles from their source, swiftly and silently, but remain largely invisible until they approach a barrier—an island or a coastline. This one originated in the Aleutian Trench 2,500 miles to the north. In only five hours it reached Hilo, causing the Hawaiian Islands' worst-ever natural disaster—in which 159 people died and damage totaled more than 25 million dollars. Vulnerable in mid-ocean, the islands have endured seven tsunami with waves at least 15 feet high since 1924. One in 1960, born of an earthquake off Chile, flattened parking meters along Kamehameha Avenue (opposite, lower) in downtown Hilo, where waves towered 35 feet.

Forces of nature—reproduced in the laboratory—yield their secrets to Japanese scientists, among the world's leaders in seismological research. At right, waves in a long, narrow tank, here operated by Professor Nobuo Shuto in Sendai, mimic the hydraulics of tsunami. Though now replaced by a computer, the tank helped researchers understand the phenomenon. The speed and height of an ocean wave, they found, depend upon water depth: For example, a ten-foot-high wave traveling through the open sea at 500 miles an hour would become a 100-foot killer when slowing to 30 miles an hour as it approached shore. At the Building Research Institute in Tsukuba (below), home of the world's largest facility for earthquake study, a technician maps every crack in a concrete test wall subjected to a simulated tremor. Also at the institute, geotechnical engineer Tsutomu Hirade (lower right) checks sensors embedded in a block of silica gel. Controlled vibrations in the gel simulate the effects of shock waves on newly made land.

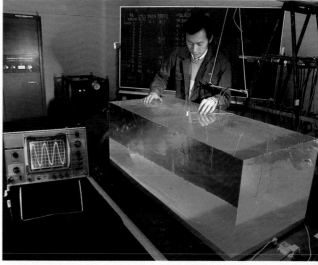

Nightmarish end to a Colombian city: Mud and debris cover Armero after the eruption of Nevado del Ruiz in November 1985. The city once sprawled over much of the valley floor, where today only a few trees and damaged homes remain visible. The volcanic spasm, though small, melted snow and ice on the mountain's summit, causing a mudflow— called a lahar—that swept over the town after most residents had gone to bed. It took more than 20,000 lives. Known for its crops of cotton and rice and its coffee warehouses, Armero owed much of its former prosperity to the mountain: An eruption in 1845 deposited millions of tons of mud on surrounding slopes. The rich topsoil supported the lush coffee plantations and farms that attracted residents to the area. At right, Nevado del Ruiz, with 90 percent of its ice cap still intact, fumes above the city of Manizales a few days after the eruption. A year later, the volcano continued to show signs of erupting again.

Submerged to her neck in the horror that was Armero, 13-year-old Omayra Sanchez clings to life as rescuers work to free her. She told them that she could feel, in the muck beneath her, the bodies of dead relatives, but she worried that the disaster would make her miss school. Below, a muddied survivor emerges from the wreckage of his home. Workers, hampered by lack of heavy equipment, pulled hundreds from the debris, but many thousands lie entombed forever. Brave Omayra, after 60 hours in the water, died of exposure leading to heart failure before rescue attempts could succeed.

ANTHONY SUAU / BLACK STAR (ABOVE AND BELOW)   A. TANNENBAUM / SYGMA

In the aftermath of the Armero disaster, a helicopter lifts one victim to safety; another (left) makes his way across the treacherous mud, more than ten feet deep in places. Relief agencies around the world dispatched aid to Colombia. U.S. search-and-rescue helicopters came from Panama; even Mexico, reeling from an earthquake that had just devastated the capital, established a mobile aid station. A medic (opposite, upper) administers tetanus and typhoid shots to survivors.

As relief efforts proceeded, questions arose: Why were the people of Armero caught unprepared? Why weren't they evacuated? As early as September, instruments detected tremors in the mountain, and escaping steam and sulfur also signaled renewed activity. Some worried residents were ready to leave, but even with volcanic ash raining down on Armero, local officials urged calm, for the time being. Said one U.S. geologist, "The volcano erupted too soon."

From quiescence to cataclysm: A sequence of unique photographs taken on May 18, 1980, captures the initial moments of the eruption of Mount St. Helens. An ominous bulge on the Washington volcano's north slope (top photo), moving as much as five feet a day, had alerted scientists to a possible major eruption. Early that morning, a magnitude-5 earthquake loosened the bulge (middle photo) and sent more than half a cubic mile of rock and ice sliding down the mountain. Hot gases, released explosively from the new crater, carried debris outward at hurricane velocities (lower photo), leveling some 250

*square miles of forest. Subsequent explosions
sent hundreds of millions of tons of ash and
pulverized rock as high as the stratosphere.
Prevailing winds bore ash eastward across
Washington and neighboring states and
provinces, darkening the sky with a black,
roiling vision from another world.*

Keeping an eye on Mount St. Helens, Gene Iwatsubo and John Ewert of the U.S. Geological Survey (opposite) use an electronic distance meter and a theodolite to monitor the growth of a new dome inside the crater. The eruption, though catastrophic, created a convenient new laboratory for volcanology and other sciences. Below, botanist Jack Lyford of Oregon State University investigates mosses that have colonized an area of steaming fumaroles a few miles from the crater. Within months, ferns, fireweed, and asters had reappeared amid the devastation, and within a year elk had returned to the Toutle River Valley. Noble fir seedlings (left) poke promising greenery out of the mud two years after the eruption. The entire ecosystem could reestablish itself in perhaps 200 years.

GARY BRAASCH (ABOVE, BOTH); RALPH PERRY (OPPOSITE); JACK HASH (FOLLOWING PAGES)

FOLLOWING PAGES: A series of incandescent rockfalls from Mount St. Helens' expanding dome appears as a molten streak in a time exposure taken at night in 1984. Eventually, the mountain may rebuild its lost summit; or further explosions may occur; or the volcano could lapse anew into a long quiet period.

Fickle Winds, Wayward Weather

by Cynthia Russ Ramsay

*"The sun flared down
on the growing corn
day after day until a line
of brown
spread along the edge
of each green bayonet.
The clouds appeared,
and went away,
and in a while they did not
try any more....
The surface of
the earth crusted,
a thin hard crust....
In the water-cut gullies
the earth dusted down
in dry little streams....*

*'Every moving thing lifted
the dust into the air...'*

—John Steinbeck,
The Grapes of Wrath

The long drought in the 1930s that turned much of the Great Plains into a dust bowl was as brutal in fact as it was in John Steinbeck's fiction. Spring and summer rains failed again and again through most of the decade, shriveling crops in fields once considered part of the nation's breadbasket.

In 1937 not a head of wheat matured in 250,000 acres sown in Cimarron County, Oklahoma. The year before, Haskell County, Kansas, produced a meager 171,000 bushels of wheat against a yield of 3.4 million in 1931. In Texas, there were no harvests in Moore County in 1935, and the Panhandle was so barren that crows were said to be building nests of barbed wire.

Cattle bawled with hunger in withered pastures. Milk cows went dry. Hogs were so scrawny no buyers would take them. Ponds evaporated. Streambeds were empty. And the parched, cracked earth, stripped of its natural grass cover and bare of crops, swirled up in the region's notorious winds and blew away in great clouds of dust.

Millions of tons of topsoil were swept up into awesome "rollers" thousands of feet high that brought a daytime darkness to the plains. In his book *Dust Bowl*, Donald Worster quotes a Kansas reporter who had been engulfed in one of those dusters in 1935: "Lady Godiva could ride thru streets without even the horse seeing her." Indoors, people slept with damp washcloths over their faces and tried to lie still "because every turn stirs the dust on the blankets." Worster also recounts the experience of a woman quoted in the *Kansas City Times*: "All we could do ... was just sit in our dusty chairs, gaze at each other through the fog that filled the room and watch that fog settle slowly and silently, covering everything—including ourselves

—in a thick, brownish gray blanket . . . . our hair was gray and stiff and we ground dirt between our teeth."

Even as the black blizzards sent gasping thousands to hospitals, and drought left many thousands more baked out of their farms and broke, people managed to joke about the situation. They told of the motorist who came upon a ten-gallon hat sitting on a dust drift. Under it, he found a head. "Do you want a ride into town?" the motorist asked. "Thanks, but I'll make it on my own," was the reply. "I'm on a horse."

The causes of the dust bowl disaster were complex. Shortsighted farming and grazing practices over decades contributed to it, but as soil geologist Robert Ruhe of Indiana University points out, lack of moisture let the soil blow away. "If you didn't have drought conditions, it wouldn't matter how you farmed," he told me. "But if you mistreat the land and get a dry spell, the wind blows, and away she goes."

For some time, meteorologists have known in a general way what went wrong with the weather in the plains during the '30s and again in the '50s and '70s. A large high-pressure system, bringing clear skies and dry weather, stalled in the upper atmosphere above the center of the continent and blocked the moist air that normally flows up from the Gulf of Mexico.

Some meteorologists associate these three major droughts with the sunspot cycle. But a leading long-range weather forecaster, Dr. Jerome Namias of the Scripps Institution of Oceanography in La Jolla, California, thinks the dry periods in the plains were linked to vast pools of abnormally cold water in the North Pacific and North Atlantic Oceans.

"The cold waters strongly influenced the air masses above them," he told me,

"creating a pattern in the upper atmosphere that anchored the high pressure system above the plains. Then, once widespread drought set in, the dry soil reinforced and perpetuated the disasters."

Dr. Namias explained that in a drought columns of air sink—going the wrong way for clouds to form. Rainfall declines further and vegetation becomes sparser, which intensifies the drought.

Examples of such chain reactions abound in the weather cycle—in which everything is connected to everything else. The sun, sea, land, and atmosphere are constantly interacting in a system of astonishing complexity. This makes it hard to pinpoint when and where the interactions are taking place, and explains why the study of weather dynamics is so challenging to scientists.

The sun's energy sets the weather machine in motion by warming the earth, which then transfers heat to the atmosphere, where the weather is made. But some parts of the earth absorb more energy than others. The Equator receives two and a half times as much solar radiation as the Poles; continents warm up and cool off more quickly than oceans; snow and ice reflect 75 percent or more of the sunlight back into space; dry sand returns about 25 percent, and dense forests as little as 5 percent. The seasons also produce sharp differences in temperature. Clouds, volcanic dust, and industrial pollution all vary the amount of solar energy reaching the earth.

The unequal heating of the atmosphere brews the world's weather, as global winds circulate in an endless effort to bring the planet's temperatures into balance. Winds are generated when warm air rises and expands, and cooler, denser air sinks and flows in to take its place. This

Complex in cause and far-reaching in effect, radical shifts in weather may reflect normal patterns or catastrophic aberrations. Across the monsoon belt (green), extremes of aridity and rainfall alternate seasonally, the result of global heat exchanges that move warm air to colder regions and cool air to hotter ones.

During the winter monsoon, prevailing winds blow south from Asia; the moisture they gather at sea drenches northeast-facing shores. Summer brings the monsoon's reversal—and respite to the parched plains of Asia and Africa. But the monsoon may also play a part in the climatic phenomenon

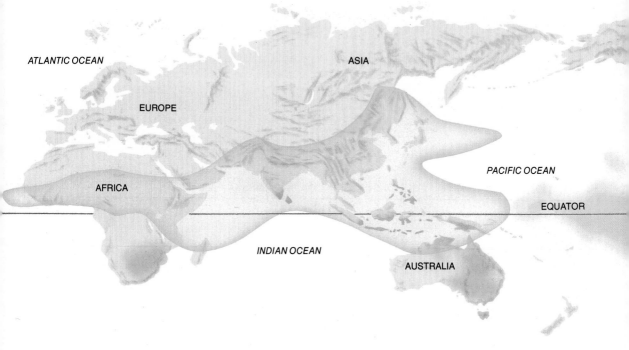

ATLANTIC OCEAN

ASIA

EUROPE

PACIFIC OCEAN

AFRICA

EQUATOR

INDIAN OCEAN

AUSTRALIA

convection occurs on a massive scale as air in the tropics rises and moves toward the Poles, and polar air plunges toward the Equator. The air currents don't travel due north or due south because the earth's rotation deflects them to their right in the Northern Hemisphere and to their left in the Southern Hemisphere. Mountains, lakes, and other variations in the landscape affect air circulation, creating countless eddies that jumble the pattern further.

The jet stream above North America is one of the giant, high-altitude rivers of air hundreds of miles wide that undulate around the globe at speeds as great as 300 miles an hour.

"These circulations are not nice steady flows; they are unstable currents, always meandering like a river pressing against its

called El Niño, which develops when Pacific trade winds falter. Its consequences in 1982-83 rank among the greatest natural disasters in recent times. El Niño resulted in drought on four continents (gold), major flooding on two (brown), and ocean warming (blue) that disrupted fisheries off South America.

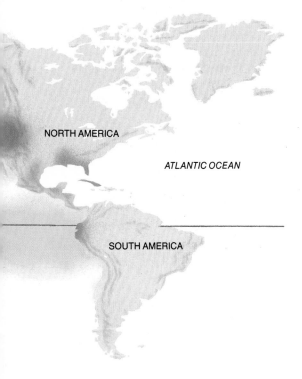

NORTH AMERICA

ATLANTIC OCEAN

SOUTH AMERICA

banks. Only there are no banks in the atmosphere, so the meanders move a lot more," said Dr. J. Murray Mitchell, veteran climatologist with the National Oceanic and Atmospheric Administration (NOAA). "We understand pretty well why the jet stream follows a winding path, but it's less clear why that path strays the way it does from month to month and year to year."

The instability and turbulence of the atmosphere led meteorologist Edward N. Lorenz of the Massachusetts Institute of Technology to wonder if the flutter of a butterfly's wings in Brazil might cause a tornado in Texas. This may not be all that farfetched. A single disturbance *can* ripple through the atmosphere, multiplying its effects many times along the way. For instance, to make a forecast for Washington,

D.C., five days in advance, a meteorologist needs to know if people are wearing galoshes in Beijing or sweltering in Cairo. "The weather anywhere on the globe is influenced by weather conditions half a world away a few days earlier," said Dr. Eugene M. Rasmusson, a climatologist who has spent most of his career with NOAA.

When the restless winds don't follow their usual patterns, they bring about freakish weather—cold snaps, unseasonable heat, too much rain or too little. When the jet stream loops far to the south in winter, a tongue of polar air funnels in—and Florida's orange crop freezes. During a prolonged dip southward over the Pacific in February 1986, the jet stream hurled torrential storm systems at California.

Wayward weather has always plagued mankind—from the biblical flood and the "dearth over all the land of Egypt" to the deluges and droughts of today. In 1315, for example, incessant rains rotted crops all over Europe and, in the words of historian Barbara Tuchman, "famine, the dark horseman of the Apocalypse, became familiar to all." From the 14th century into the 1800s, Europe was frequently beset by cold, wet summers. Poor wheat harvests led to food riots in France and England and mass starvation in Scotland and Finland. Germans and Italians resorted to eating snakes, cats, and dogs. Norwegians sustained themselves on tree bark and bread containing bark and lichens.

University of Wisconsin climatologist Reid A. Bryson describes these disasters in terms of a shift in the summer track of the jet stream. According to Dr. Bryson, the jet stream changed course and took a path at a lower latitude. Cold polar air pushed farther south, ushering in what is now referred to as the little ice age.

But even then there were some warm, dry spells. In September 1666, when the Great Fire raged through London, Samuel Pepys noted in his diary, "everything, after so long a drought, proving combustible, even the very stones of churches."

An abnormally wet spring and summer in Ireland in 1846 encouraged the spread of the blight that destroyed the entire potato crop. Thousands died in the famine that followed—too many, clergymen reported, for individual funerals to be held. Describing the human misery, one historian writes: "The worst sufferers were the children . . . many too far gone to be able to walk. . . . looking like little old men and women . . . wrinkled and bent."

Archaeologists and other scientists have found evidence for recurrent droughts in the American Southwest. Tree rings, wide in wet years and narrow in dry ones, point to a major dry spell that lasted from 1276 to 1299—the period in which the Anasazi Indians began abandoning their great pueblo communities. Dr. Bryson thinks that drought also may have hastened the end of the Mycenaean civilization in Greece and the Harappan in the Indus Valley, as well as the Mill Creek farming culture in what is now Iowa.

Drought strikes at more people than any other natural disaster. Few places escape it altogether. Even umbrella-toting Londoners faced 16 virtually rainless months during the drought of 1975-76—possibly the worst in the city's history. In the south of England crops failed, rivers shrank or even dwindled away, and industries were on the verge of shutdown.

Almost every year parts of the United States suffer drought. In California in 1976-77, wells and reservoirs dried up; water rationing was imposed on communities in the San Francisco Bay area; and irrigation sprinklers were turned off in the hard-hit Central Valley. The disaster cost farmers more than a billion dollars. The culprit was the jet stream. It steered the Hawaiian high-pressure system north of its usual location, blocking rain-bearing storms that normally reach California.

Dr. Mitchell believes the drought also

may have been tied to the sunspot cycle. "Sunspots are huge magnetic storms that pock the face of the sun," he said. "Their numbers rise and fall every 11 years. But it takes two 11-year cycles to bring the sun's magnetic field back to its starting configuration. Every 22 years, when sunspot activity is at a low point, widespread drought is especially favored to break out somewhere in the West. The plains droughts of the '30s and '50s and the West Coast drought of the '70s were in phase with this 22-year cycle.

"It's true there have been many will-o'-the-wisp correlations between sunspots and weather that are hard to substantiate as advertised. The problem is we don't know what to look for; we don't know what the chain of cause and effect is."

The meanderings of the jet stream in 1985 were linked to the failure of rains in the Northeast and a drought that turned eastern Montana as "brown and bald as a steer's back." In Alberta and Saskatchewan, ditches filled with blown dirt; maples and poplars lost their leaves in summer; crops were scorched; and the ground looked as gray and lifeless as an ash heap. Farmers suggested giving preachers raises so that they would pray harder for rain.

"Wheat is one of the hardiest plants. One shower would have at least gotten our seed back," said farmer William Giblett of Bengough, Saskatchewan. "But mother nature turned off the tap. Even with advanced technology, when she turns mean, you're pretty helpless."

In 1986 the jet stream looped off course again, and a huge rain-blocking high-pressure cell persisted over the Southeast. Farmers anxiously scanned the skies for signs of rain as they watched their fields parch and burn. Cottonseeds planted in April lay in the ground for two months without sprouting—as dormant as if they had been sitting in a warehouse. Soybeans, which should have been waist-high in July, stood just inches above the ground. Corn was stunted, too, and no ears grew on the withered stalks.

Heat records melted away as hundred-degree days became common in the Carolinas and Georgia. Midway through the summer, rainfall was less than half of normal in many counties. "Our topsoil usually holds a tremendous amount of moisture that evaporates and gives us our thunderstorms," said Dave Smith, agricultural meteorologist with the National Weather Service at Clemson, South Carolina. "The ground was so dry we even lost this local, secondary source of moisture. It's a case of positive feedback—a bad situation breeding conditions that make it worse."

The scorched earth created tinderbox conditions that contributed to hundreds of forest fires. It had not been so dry in more than a hundred years.

*I*n the tropics, the monsoon is the chief mechanism for bringing or withholding rain. Much of Africa and Asia lives at the mercy of this seasonal wind, called monsoon after the Arabic word for season. This major weather phenomenon occurs in latitudes where the sun's rays are the strongest. The land heats up in the blazing sun, while ocean temperatures lag far behind. The sharp contrast generates wide-ranging sea breezes laden with moisture and the promise of rain. As the ocean air sweeps inland over the heated countryside, it expands, becomes lighter, rises, and cools. When the air is sufficiently cool, its vapor condenses into billowing clouds. Massive updrafts constantly draw ocean air into these circulations that keep half of mankind from starvation.

But occasionally the monsoon arrives late, or leaves early, or simply fizzles out. Dr. Jagadish Shukla, a meteorologist at the University of Maryland, has been trying to discover why the monsoon sometimes falters in India. Like many of his colleagues, he works with huge computers that use mathematical models to simulate the atmosphere and the weather. Through his experiments Dr. Shukla has found that if the surface waters of the Indian Ocean and the Pacific are warmer, it rains more over the oceans, and the monsoon rains over land are reduced. His research also suggests that snow cover over a broad area in Eurasia—from the Alps to Siberia— tends to weaken the monsoon.

When the monsoon fails, so do crops planted in anticipation of rain. People grow weak from hunger, and large numbers of them die. In countries where the majority lives close to the edge of survival, drought spells famine. The monsoon that bypassed parts of China in 1877 caused disaster on a horrendous scale—claiming an estimated 10 to 13 million lives. Millions more perished in India during the widespread droughts of 1770, 1877, and 1899. Unreliable rains have long plagued Ethiopia, which suffered its first recorded famine in the ninth century.

In recent years the failure of the monsoon has condemned much of Africa to punishing drought. Fields have turned to dust, pastures into wastelands, rivers into shrunken streams, and multitudes into walking skeletons. Neither the African governments nor the international relief agencies know exactly how many have died. No reliable statistics exist for the numbers who have perished in nomad tents hundreds of miles from the nearest town and in isolated villages two days' walk from the nearest dirt road. Some reports state that within the last 15 years more than a million Africans have died of starvation and disease. But even such grim figures do not convey the true dimensions of the catastrophe. That story is told by the sad eyes of children, by proud nomads reduced to begging, by the hellish sounds of parents grieving, and by the thousands upon thousands of refugees wandering across the parched land. It is told by the little boy of six or seven who eats a piece of bread crumb by crumb because he is afraid it will soon be gone and he will be hungry again.

"He was so small, and he knew that terrible hunger," said India's Mother Teresa, speaking at a refugee camp in Ethiopia. In a lifetime among the destitute, she had seen nothing like the famine in that country. She called it an "open Calvary," where perhaps 10,000 were crucified nightly.

It was absolute desperation that drove the Ethiopian farmers from fields that had been in their families for generations. Laura Kullenberg, a program director for the Oxfam relief agency, described for me the

El Niño—The Child—tends to begin during the Christmas season. Then, South American fishermen sometimes notice an unusual warming of Pacific coastal waters. Normally, trade winds blow west (upper diagram) toward a warm, rainy low-pressure area near Australia and Indonesia. The trades push ocean currents along, and warm water (green) accumulates in the western Pacific. Subsurface water (blue) upwells off South America, forming a deep, nutrient-rich layer of cool water. But when the western Pacific low-pressure zone shifts eastward every few years, winds and currents stall or reverse

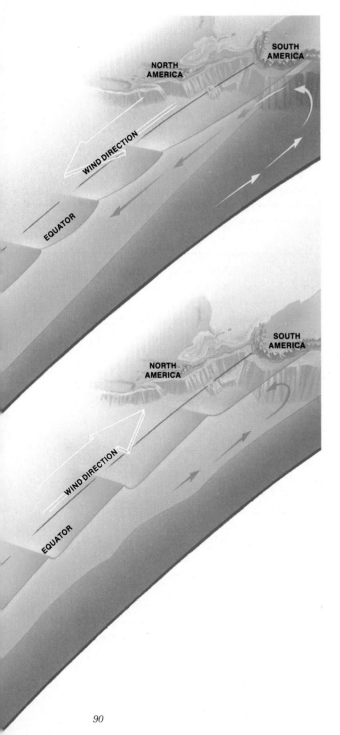

sequence of despair as the long drought tightened its grip on their lives.

"In 1981, the first year of bad rains, the farmers lived on surpluses or were able to borrow. The second year was harder, and people began selling their livestock, tools, and draft animals. They held on to family heirlooms—silver crosses and jewelry—as long as they could. By the third year, the pastures had dried up, but still they waited, hoping the rains would come. By 1984 they had sold everything—their cooking pots, even the thatch off their roofs—and had only the tattered clothes on their backs. When there was nothing left, those who were not too weak to move walked off in search of food."

Laura, then only 28, had been sent to Ethiopia in November 1984, at the height of the emergency, to determine what supplies were needed at refugee camps and in the villages. Foreign governments were providing food. She encountered a stream of anguished humanity moving along a road about a hundred miles north of the capital of Addis Ababa.

"They were half dazed," she said. "Some had been walking for days; many had had nothing to eat but leaves for weeks. Children would kneel down in front of our car to stop us. They saw us as their last hope.

"I had been schooled in the reality that we have to go about relief work in an organized, methodical way. I was not prepared for what I saw."

The world became aware of Ethiopia's agony in the last months of 1984 and was shocked into action by press reports and television images. The outpouring of aid to the more than seven million Ethiopians in need was unprecedented. Those starving in Sudan and in the countries of the Sahel

direction—and El Niño results (lower). Rain diminishes in Australia and southern Asia; freak storms may pound Pacific islands and the Americas' west coast. When severe, El Niño can affect even larger areas—not surprisingly, since the area where it originates spans a quarter of the globe.

received less publicity, but their suffering was just as intolerable.

The Sahel is an immense, sandy plain dotted with thornbushes and acacia trees that stretches along the southern fringes of the Sahara. Even in the best of times, little rain falls on the Sahel. Whatever comes is brought by the monsoon from June to September. Since 1968, precipitation has been well below normal, and 1983 and 1984 were the driest years of the century. Clouds of red dust were swept up into the atmosphere; soil particles, rich in iron oxide, were carried across the Atlantic, and for several summers red mud fell on Miami, Florida. The calamity in the Sahel, meteorologists say, is the longest, most devastating drought of modern times.

In 1985 monsoon rains improved over much of stricken Africa, though rainfall was still below normal. Relief organizations rushed seeds to farmers who had eaten their own as a last resort, and millet, sorghum, and rice once again greened the fields around the mud-hut villages.

New grass also sprang up in the Sahel sands. But the rains did not ease the suffering of the nomads, including the 300,000 Tuareg of Mali, Niger, and Chad. For them the green pastures were a heartbreaking sight because there were practically no animals left to graze on them.

When I arrived in Mali in May 1986, the Tuareg were still overwhelmed by the effects of the drought. A tall people proud of their warrior tradition, they face a bleak future—one without the cattle, sheep, camels, and goats that once gave them meat and milk, social status, and a cherished way of life.

"Since the animals are gone, we are no more human beings," a Tuareg named Ibrahim Ag Sidi told me, speaking through the swath of turban that veiled most of his face. We were sitting in the sparse shade of a spindly acacia tree on the outskirts of Ménaka, a sun-scorched town in Mali's remote eastern corner. My companions, field-workers for the aid organization World Vision, served as our interpreters.

"Don't ask us if we have animals. If we had them, we wouldn't be here," Ibrahim said. There was no impatience in his low voice—only sorrow. "To stay in town is a punishment. But we can't leave because we don't have any animals. We are like in a prison. We have eaten everything we owned —selling our wooden bowls, silver, camel saddles. That is why we don't even have a nice carpet for you to sit on."

Ibrahim and thousands like him have no land, no resources, and few skills beyond their mastery of the desert and their ability to herd animals across the trackless sameness of the Sahel. Some Tuareg, it is said, can tell where they are by smelling and touching the sand. For centuries the Tuareg have scorned manual labor, saying, "These hands know only the sword and the camel saddle." They considered cultivating crops demeaning. It was a measure of their plight that the women of Ibrahim's family had tried to raise vegetables, but they had little success. "It's very difficult; we don't know how," one of them said.

The younger men of the family were in Ménaka, looking for work as day laborers. Ibrahim, like many refugees, earns a little money selling firewood and charcoal—at a cost to the land. Tree cutting has exposed the thin soil to wind and runoff that pirate it away. Overgrazing has done the same, hastening the spread of the desert and deepening the crisis.

Many Tuareg will not talk about the

humiliation of these hard times. "We survive with courage," one told me. "God puts a veil on our shame," said another. Some families send their children to town to scavenge. Some beg. A few peddle trinkets and family treasures. Others wait in miserable tent camps for rations of grain, powdered milk, sugar, and oil distributed by relief organizations. CARE has several Food for Work projects in Mali, but there were few Tuareg at the one I visited. "They don't know how to handle a shovel," said the African foreman, whose ancestors had been vassals of Tuareg overlords.

Still pinched by hunger, the Tuareg must make agonizing decisions about their future. Many have reluctantly decided they must abandon their life-style. They are asking help to dig wells, to grow crops, and to establish permanent settlements. Others still hope to restore their herds, as they did after the drought of 1972-73, and to resume their age-old migrations. "We want to see the footprints of people return to the open spaces," said Bajan Ag Hamatou, a deputy in Mali's National Assembly.

Disagreements over what course to follow are wrenching the clans apart. "Sometimes the sons of the same father and same mother are so angry they have decided not to talk to each other till the end of the earth," said Mohamad Ag Al Hassan. I was visiting his clan's encampment with a group from CARE. We had driven there from Timbuktu, across a roadless monotony of sand and scattered acacia trees. The sun was an intense glow in a sky hazy with dust, and in the harsh glare the sandy ground gave off heat in almost visible waves; the temperature must have been around 120°F. In late May, more than a month before the monsoon, the grasses had baked to straw, and the small leaves of the trees were gritty with sand from a recent windstorm. After a jolting 90-minute ride, we arrived at a small cluster of tents beside a well in the middle of nowhere.

That day I learned of children going to bed hungry and of animals dying by the hundred. I met mothers and wives who waited in vain to hear from men who had left more than a year before to find work in distant towns. Even once strong family ties have become casualties of the drought.

I learned that Mohamad had resigned as chief of his clan. Too many of his people wanted to settle down, and he couldn't bring himself to stop them. "It isn't easy to give orders in these times," he told me.

A few of Mohamad's animals had survived the drought, and he was determined not to surrender the freedom of the nomadic life. "Does the farmer live without risk? Is there life without risk?" he asked.

But if the decline in rainfall that began in the 1960s persists, the Sahel grasses will surely succumb to the sterile sand. Then neither Mohamad nor any other Tuareg will ever again herd his animals across the plain, and drought will have destroyed a remarkable way of life.

Many meteorologists believe the drought is a short-term fluctuation—part of a normal cycle in a region prone to dry spells. Others contend that the drought has lasted so long it reflects a long-term climatic change. The consensus among nearly all meteorologists is that no one really knows what has been keeping the monsoon from the Sahel.

"We know global circulations are to blame, but we throw up our hands when it comes to identifying the specific trigger," Eugene Rasmusson told me.

Some scientists have looked to the tropical Atlantic, the birthplace of the Sahel's monsoon, for clues. They have discerned a distinct change in sea-surface temperatures during the driest years. The zone of highest temperatures shifts 200 miles south, and a low-pressure trough—which sits over warm water and feeds water vapor into the atmosphere and into West Africa—moves with it.

Dr. Peter J. Lamb, head of the Climate and Meteorology Section of the Illinois State Water Survey, believes this displacement reduces the monsoon's reach into West Africa and allows dry northeast winds blowing off the Sahara to extend farther south.

"This shift in surface temperatures in the Atlantic can help explain why the rainy season is poor. But why the ocean temperatures change and why drought conditions have persisted for almost 20 years remains an open question," he told me.

Dr. Lamb may have separated one thread from the web of disaster, but, as Dr. Rasmusson puts it, "The ocean and the drought may both be responding to a third factor we haven't even considered yet."

There are so many random factors it's not surprising meteorologists disagree. "We're dealing with a situation a little like that of the blind men and the elephant," said Dr. Rasmusson. "The processes behind climate variability are so complex that each of us tends to focus on only a piece of the problem instead of the whole animal."

But these days few doubt that changes in sea-surface temperatures in the tropics are a major source of climate variability.

"The tropical oceans are an extremely important factor. Evaporation takes place there at the rate of several billion gallons an hour. The moisture is wicked up into great cumulonimbus clouds rising 40,000 feet and higher," Dr. Rasmusson said. "When the vapor cools and condenses into rain, energy is released into the atmosphere. So when an increase in the sea-surface temperatures induces rainfall, it is stoking the atmospheric boiler. This speeds up the subtropical jet stream and changes circulation patterns around the world."

El Niño, the warming of the surface waters of the tropical eastern Pacific, clearly illustrates the interaction between the ocean and the atmosphere. In normal years, trade winds blow steadily across the ocean from east to west, dragging warm surface water along in the same direction. This results in a shallow layer of warm water in the eastern Pacific and a buildup of warm water in the west. During El Niño, normal winds falter and ocean currents reverse. Warm water migrates to the eastern Pacific. As sea-surface temperatures there begin to rise, the heavy rains of the western equatorial Pacific also extend eastward into the normally dry region. This disrupts trade winds even more.

"We don't know what triggers those climatic flip-flops," said Dr. Rasmusson. "It could be that El Niño begins with a random shift of winds, or it may work the other way around and begin with a build-up of warm water. But most places on earth feel its effects."

Niños, like earthquakes, vary in intensity, and the one of 1982-83 was a massive aberration. It affected weather patterns on five continents. It suppressed rains in some areas, causing severe drought, and it spawned downpours in others. In the United States a succession of storms drenched the West and Gulf coasts, causing severe floods that did hundreds of millions of dollars' worth of property damage.

*F*loods are among the most destructive of natural hazards, and rarely does a year go by without a major flood somewhere in the world. The most widespread flooding in the United States occurs in the Mississippi basin, where cold, dry air from Canada frequently collides with warm, moist air from the Caribbean and the Gulf of Mexico. The warm air is lifted by the heavier cold air, which pushes under it like a wedge. The result: soaking rains.

Since 1844 the Mississippi has raged out of its banks a dozen times. In the spring of 1973, after months of unusually wet weather, the ground became saturated. Heavy runoff poured into tributaries and surged into the swollen Mississippi, which rose higher and higher. Before long it backed up the Yazoo River, submerging the Yazoo-Mississippi Delta north of Vicksburg and creating an inland sea 60 miles long and 40 miles wide. Nearly everything went underwater except Highway 61, the railroad, and the Mississippi levee.

The levee offered a dry place for animals—a modern-day Noah's ark. Deer, foxes, rabbits, raccoons, opossums, minks, and snakes assembled in remarkable proximity. Alligators got so tired of swimming they crawled up on the levee, too. Deer left the levee to feed; they swam out in the water and hooked their forelegs over branches to browse on leaves. Wild turkeys, roosting in trees, waited for the grain that people put out on barges for the animals.

For farmer Clifton Porter of Rolling Fork, Mississippi, there was no refuge. "Every morning I'd take a stick and measure how much the water had gone up in my fields," he recalled. "It was real gradual so you had time to go crazy. When it started in February, we thought we'd have water in the low spots. But it just kept on raining, and the water kept on coming. I finally moved out of my house at the end of April and every piece of farm equipment went with me. I had pictured calm, still water, but winds stirred up waves that rolled across the fields and crashed against the sides of houses. In some cases waves tore the houses apart. Other structures collapsed when the water dissolved the mortar between the bricks."

It took him six months to repair his house. "We had to shovel out the muck in the basement and deal with the mildew on the floors. The waterlogged carpets were so heavy we cut them up to haul them away. I had to rewire the house, replace the insulation, and buy new furniture."

Troubles extended far beyond the Yazoo area, for virtually the entire Mississippi system was flooded. Damages totaled one billion dollars, and 33 lives were lost.

The death toll was much higher in South Dakota on June 9, 1972, when seven inches of rain fell in six hours. Rapid Creek rampaged out of its bed and hurtled down from the Black Hills with a roar like a freight train's. It swept up automobiles and battered them against buildings as it tore through the streets of Rapid City. The debris-choked torrent splintered homes, ripped up pavements, chewed away bridges —and killed more than 200 people.

The storm started when a strong breeze from the southeast pushed a mass of moist air against the Black Hills and caused it to rise and release its moisture. Conditions in the upper atmosphere made matters worse; the winds were unusually light and did not disperse the moist air. And the steepness of the terrain gave the deluge its death-dealing velocity.

Such random combinations have resulted in calamitous blizzards that have immobilized large sections of the country. More than 400 died (200 in New York City alone) in the great blizzard of 1888, which paralyzed the Northeast from Washington, D.C., to Boston. NOAA writer Patrick Hughes tracked down some of the details of the disaster, which began with rain on a mild Sunday afternoon in March and ended with 40 to 50 inches of snow and drifts 40 feet high. In his book *American Weather Stories*, Hughes reports that the blizzard sank or wrecked 200 vessels in offshore waters and "buried trains all over the Northeast." In Brooklyn "more than 20 letter carriers were found unconscious in snowdrifts." On Long Island 30 funeral processions were stalled, and the coffins had to be kept in nearby houses overnight. Throughout the Northeast, telegraph and telephone lines broke under the weight of ice and snow or snapped in the wind. The most populous section of the country was cut off from the world.

Hughes points out that as a result of the storm, most of the region's telegraph and telephone lines were put underground. Otherwise, much that he describes—deserted streets, snowbound trains, stranded travelers, abandoned vehicles (in this case, horse-drawn streetcars)—could apply to the storm that ripped through the Northeast 90 years later.

A 40-hour storm in February 1978 dumped 17.7 inches of snow on New York, and once again the city was brought to a standstill, its stores and businesses closed and transportation crippled. The swirling

FOLLOWING PAGES: Forced from their homes by hunger, victims of African drought crowd a refugee camp in Ethiopia. By 1984, the failure of several rainy seasons caused the devastating drought that helped bring on one of the most pervasive famines in the continent's history. Booming populations,

flakes silenced the streets, dispersed the crowds, and buried the trash and litter under a blanket of white.

Other cities were battered as well. Thousands of cars were stranded on highways around Boston, and I saw Washington, D.C., turn into a ghost town. Panic over the forecast for heavy snow emptied offices and briefly crowded supermarkets with people stocking up for the siege. By morning roads were obliterated, schools were closed, and the pavements belonged to skiers. No one could doubt that weather rules our lives.

But something new has been added to the multitude of variables in the weather equation. Man is now changing the composition of the atmosphere. The destruction of tropical forests worldwide and the burning of fossil fuels by industries and automobiles have increased the carbon dioxide content by about 20 percent in the last century. The CO_2 produces greenhouse conditions, trapping some of the heat that would otherwise escape into space. The buildup of CO_2 and trace gases such as those used in refrigeration and in aerosol sprays can amplify the greenhouse effect.

Scientists debate the long-term consequences if this buildup continues. A warmer earth could melt the polar ice, raising sea levels and swamping coastlines. Global circulations could change, altering rainfall patterns. Or cloudiness could increase and offset the greenhouse effect.

Weather and its phenomena are so complex we should not expect simple answers. But as I pray for snow to ski on in winter, for spring showers to make the wildflowers bloom in Virginia, and for timely rains for beleaguered Africa, I must also pray that wayward weather does not become the rule rather than the exception.

civil strife, and unwise agricultural practices compounded the tragedy. Countries suffered extensive crop and livestock losses. In Ethiopia, tens of thousands of people died of starvation or disease. Estimates of the toll in Mozambique, to the south, also ranged into the thousands. But few areas of the continent remained unaffected; the drought ravaged nearly 30 nations and touched 150 million people in a broad crescent stretching from Senegal and Mauritania to South Africa. Life-giving rains finally returned in 1985, bringing with them guarded hopes for an end to Africa's recurrent nightmare.

Race against time slows to a snail's pace in the desert of Sudan as men clear tracks for a relief-laden convoy. Even after emergency aid began arriving in Africa in the 1980s, delivering it to the needy proved a formidable task. Grain and other supplies piled up at major ports and airfields because of the scarcity of trucks and fuel. And often no roads existed to link such depots with remote villages and feeding camps. Guarding against marauders, military escorts accompanied the first trucks to reach the camp at Korem, where 50,000 desperate Ethiopians from the surrounding countryside waited. Among them: the listless youngsters at right, who survived. More at risk from malnutrition than adults, the young often succumbed to common childhood diseases. Another problem, unforeseen, illustrated the tragedy's extent: Relief workers at many camps reported that some children had to be hand-fed; they had forgotten how to eat.

Quest for water becomes a life-or-death mission across drought-stricken Africa. A four-day trek brings nomads and their camels to a public well in Somalia (opposite); as if to underscore nature's cruel caprices, a dust devil churns beyond. Resettlement projects for Somalia's nomadic majority feature irrigation systems, but near one such village a dry riverbed idles the pumps (bottom). Near Timbuktu, in Mali (below), sticks serve as tools to beat clay into the sides of a new irrigation canal. Much of Mali lies within the dry Sahel, parts of which average less than seven inches of rainfall a year.

MICHAEL S. YAMASHITA (ABOVE AND OPPOSITE); CYNTHIA RUSS RAMSAY, N.G.S. STAFF (TOP)

Moving walls of flame, as high as 30 feet, pit fire fighters against a goliath of western wildfires in California's Los Padres National Forest, northwest of Los Angeles. Working round the clock through the 1985 Fourth of July holiday, nearly 3,000 professionals and volunteers kept the blaze from the nearby town of Ojai, but the deflected flames eventually consumed 118,000 acres of woodland and chaparral. At right, fire fighters work a break—a strip cleared to stop the flames' advance. Though the Ojai fire, which burned for two weeks, ranked as one of the summer's most stubborn, a two-year drought combined with abnormally high temperatures and low humidity to turn much of the West into a tinderbox; by fall, fires had laid waste more than a million acres in 14 states and British Columbia. Ironically, the warm, dry weather that preceded them favored outdoor recreation and the kind of human carelessness responsible for many major blazes.

FOLLOWING PAGES: Smoke casts an ashen pall over the landscape as heat from the Ojai fire forms billowing clouds. Charred slopes lie vulnerable to erosion and mud slides.

RICHARD MACKSON (ABOVE, OPPOSITE, AND FOLLOWING PAGES)

Flood follows fire in February 1986, as California receives its heaviest drenching in years. To blame: an inexplicable mid-Pacific split in the jet stream, a high-altitude air current that influences much of North America's weather. Its southern branch, dubbed the "Pineapple Express," bore cargoes of tropical moisture to California, spawning a series of violent storms. Fire-scarred areas like those around Ojai had long expected mud slides and washouts. Above, a pickup negotiates an angry torrent in

Ojai's East End. By the time Matilija Canyon Road (above, right) became impassable, the neighborhood had been evacuated. Storms also battered northern California, where major rivers overflowed and levees crumbled after several days of steady rain. At right, a street's name mocks its condition in the town of Rio Vista near the Sacramento River.

FOLLOWING PAGES: Last trace of Interstate 5, the Twin Cities Road overpass in San Joaquin County barely escapes submersion.

JAMES A. SUGAR (BELOW AND FOLLOWING PAGES); GEORGE OLSON (ABOVE, BOTH)

Drifts rise and weather records fall in Buffalo, New York, one of the country's snowiest major cities. Below, residents shovel their way out after a typical snowstorm in January 1983. In December 1985, a mountain of snow dwarfs ten-foot street signs—and Stanley Buczkowski, Buffalo's undaunted streets

commissioner. New snow is also old news to another resident, Mrs. Stella Helinski, who takes the situation sitting down. Snow fell on all but two days that December, totaling 68.4 inches and breaking the monthly snowfall record set in January 1977. Why does Buffalo bear winter's brunt— with about a hundred inches of white stuff a year? The city's location near vast bodies of water makes it a prime target for the "lake effect," as frigid blasts from north and west gather moisture over the Great Lakes and then dump it as snow on their leeward shores.

Wind-roiled snow paints a Minnesota farmstead in chilly monochrome. Far from the news-making turmoil of cities under blizzards' siege, rural areas often suffer more acute and wide-ranging consequences from harsh winter weather. Late snowstorms that disrupt spring planting schedules may portend disaster in critically important farm belts, such as the Great Plains or the Siberian wheat lands. Despite improved forecasting and airlifts of feed grain, blizzards still imperil livestock; one plains storm in 1975 cost cattlemen 56,000 calves. In some northern regions, agricultural practices

actually increase winter's threats to animals.
In a Minnesota wildlife management area,
wildlife specialist Roy Peterson (left) holds
a pheasant suffocated by ice. The state's
pheasant population declines as woodlots
and cattail marshes—where the birds find
winter shelter—are converted to cropland.

Brevity of summer monsoon rains lends urgency to the task of a rice planter in Nepal. Like half of Asia's farmers, he depends on the rains for a single growing season. A gift of the gods, they prove as fickle—flooding here, failing there in unpredictable sequence. Or they bless and curse simultaneously, washing away fertile soil that makes a waterfall in India rage toffee-brown (opposite).

FOLLOWING PAGES: At most an inconvenience, wall-to-wall water carpets a home in the Indonesian city of Bojonegoro, swept by floods during the winter monsoon of 1984.

STEVE McCURRY (BELOW, OPPOSITE, AND FOLLOWING PAGES)

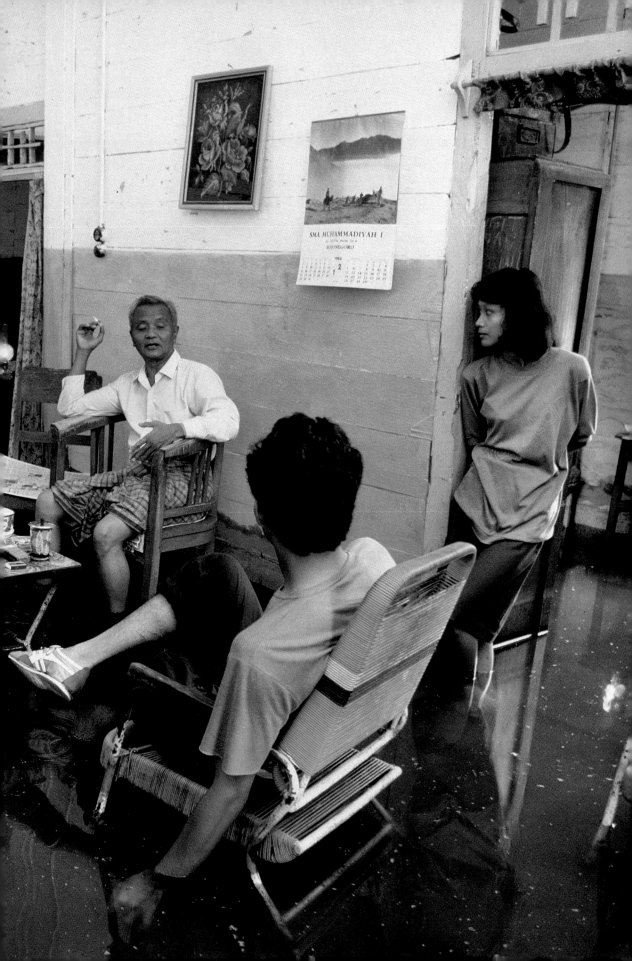

Whirlwinds and Thunderbolts

by Gene S. Stuart

"...during a winter's night,
about six o'clock
in the evening,
there arose a wind,
which kept increasing and
soon changed into
a hurricane of four winds.

This wind overthrew
all the large trees causing
a great destruction
of every kind of game;
and it destroyed
also all the tall
houses which, since they
were covered with straw
and contained fire
on account of the cold,
were set on fire,
and they burned up
a large part of the people."

—Diego de Landa,
Relation of the Things of Yucatán

Thus wrote Bishop Diego de Landa in 1566, setting down in vivid detail the stories native Maya Indians told him of a devastating storm that had swept Mexico's Yucatán Peninsula several generations before. "This hurricane lasted till the next day at noon," the Maya related. Observing the area's subsequent recovery and the uniform regrowth of forest, the Spanish bishop noted: "in casting one's eyes over the country from some high points, it looks as if the whole had been cut off by scissors." Modern scholars believe the storm had occurred about a hundred years before Landa heard the stories—possibly in 1464, making it the earliest reported hurricane in the New World.

Carib Indians, who lived near Yucatán and gave their name to the Caribbean Sea and its islands, called such a violent storm *huracan* for their god of hurricanes and thunderbolts. The ancient Quiché Maya of Guatemala worshiped Huracan, or Heart of Sky, a fearsome creator-destroyer deity who caused torrential rainstorms, possibly hurricanes, and may have been a personification of the unleashed forces of nature. Spaniards borrowed the word and accented it as *huracán*, naming storms unknown in Spain but all too common in parts of the New World. English speakers adapted the word to their tongue. Huracán or hurricane—the words still evoke dread and portend destruction.

Spanish colonial chronicles of the Maya mention that hurricanes of extreme intensity also ravaged the Yucatán Peninsula in 1560 and 1661, and then again in 1766. Modern records show that in September 1955 Janet, one of the fiercest hurricanes in history, struck the same area with winds of about 200 miles an hour, leaving few buildings intact and uprooting enormous trees. Some 500 people died in Quintana Roo, the Mexican state that stretches along the peninsula's east coast. Janet must have been comparable to the horrendous storm of 1464.

In the late summer of 1974, while on an archaeological expedition in Quintana Roo, my family and I lived in Cobá, a modern Maya village built within the ruins of an ancient Maya city some 15 miles inland. Our house, like the others scattered along the shore of a lake, was of ancient Maya design, with walls of saplings lashed together with vines and set into a dirt floor, and a roof thatched with cabbage-palm leaves. During the afternoon of September 1, nature began repeating its dread pattern.

A steady drizzle early that day had come as no surprise, for the annual rainy season usually lingers into September. But as afternoon stretched toward evening, the increasing downpour and the violent gusts in a growing tempest gave us anxious pause. By the time darkness came, the rain fell in torrents and the wind blew with such fury that it caused those who ventured outdoors to lean and lurch and to place each foot so carefully they seemed to be climbing invisible ladders. A neighbor who owned a radio spread the news through the village: A hurricane was approaching the coast and would make landfall sometime during the night.

The lake had already risen, and water covered the only road leading out through the forest that surrounded us. Since there was no escape and no better choice of shelter than our house, we bolted the door, secured window shutters, and observed our normal evening routine. I lit the kerosene lamps (ironically, hurricane lanterns) and managed to prepare a meal over the cooking fire that burned in the middle of the

floor. Each of us slung a hammock and mosquito netting beneath heavy log beams and, as usual, extinguished lanterns and bedded down early. The fire died out. We waited and we listened.

No night is as dark as a tropical night without moon or stars. No sound is as awesome on such a night as the thunderous pandemonium of nature on the rampage. Wind swirled through the forest, and trees thrashed about as if in battle. Our pole walls proved no deterrent to fierce winds that drove rain through one end of the house almost horizontally. Inside, wind and rain spun our mosquito netting around us until we hung enveloped in sodden gauze cocoons. The house swayed and shuddered in the strongest gusts and assumed altered shapes, while vines and beams moaned with the strain of it. At times we spoke assurances to one another. Once, we disentangled ourselves from netting, lit lanterns, and stood silently watching and listening to the sounds of the storm. Each hour seemed endless, but by morning the worst winds abated; then a gentle breeze blew, and we slept.

Late morning brought sunshine and serenity. Trees glistened and dripped from the deluge, but none had been uprooted. No one in the village reported injury. After a night spent inside our crazed parallelogram of a house, we checked for damage. Rain had soaked through most of our possessions, but not a palm leaf had been displaced, not a pole stood out of line.

We discovered that a refugee from the hurricane had joined us during the night; just inside the door an enormous toad sat motionless, trying to conceal itself behind a Pepsi-Cola bottle that somehow remained upright; it measured only half the terrified toad's width. We never learned how the animal managed to get inside; perhaps massive strength inspired by fear had enabled it to squeeze through a narrow opening in the wall.

For toad and humans alike the worst fears of that long night lay in not knowing what to expect. Without a radio in the house, my family and I did not hear broadcasts of warnings hours ahead, but faced our ordeal as poorly prepared as those hapless Maya some 500 years before. In the following days details gradually came to light, giving the storm a distinct identity.

Her name was Carmen, and she began life off the west coast of Africa in late August. Nurtured by her long journey across the open Atlantic, she gained strength by drawing heat from the warm water. Carmen swept small Caribbean islands and spawned a tornado, heavy rains, and flash floods in Puerto Rico. Picking up speed and force over open water once more, the storm hurtled toward Yucatán—potentially one of the worst hurricanes in recent history, as devastating as Janet.

Capricious like most hurricanes, Carmen veered slightly to the north. As she made landfall, her southern semicircle swept Chetumal, Quintana Roo's capital. There she bore sustained winds of 130 miles an hour or more. Her northern half, the area packing even stronger winds and powerful gusts, battered the area of Cobá. The hurricane peaked before dawn on September 2, and later, in the morning gloom, the hurricane-force winds weakened over Quintana Roo.

Crossing the peninsula, Carmen headed north into the Gulf of Mexico, regained hurricane force, and on September 7 struck the Louisiana coast. People there heeded the dire warnings: Some 100,000 fled their homes. Although damage by Carmen has

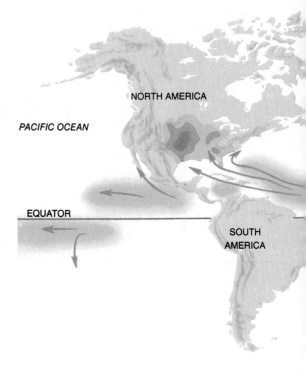

been estimated at 130 million dollars, authorities reported only three deaths; three had died in the Yucatán Peninsula as well.

The U.S. National Weather Service announced that disaster had been avoided in Mexico because "the major part of Carmen's fury was expended over the undeveloped and thinly populated part of the Yucatán Peninsula north of Chetumal." From within that small population, human (and possibly toad) disdain at the seemingly callous announcement went unnoticed. But a catastrophe indeed had been averted: in Cobá, by good fortune alone; in Louisiana, by expert reporting and planning.

Huracán, hurricane, cyclone, typhoon, or, in the Philippines, *bagyo:* The word varies depending on locale, but all refer to the same thing—a revolving tropical storm

little more than a football field and spins itself out after six miles. Hurricanes span hundreds of miles and sweep over oceans and coastlines. In an average year six tropical storms build to hurricane strength in the Atlantic. Tropic seas of summer provide the necessary ingredients—heat and humidity.

Whirling about low-pressure cores, hurricanes (blue arrows) drift with the trade winds, then curve toward the poles of their hemispheres. Colliding air masses breed an annual fury of twisters in North America— especially in the Midwest's "Tornado Alley"; colors indicate frequency, from light to heavy.

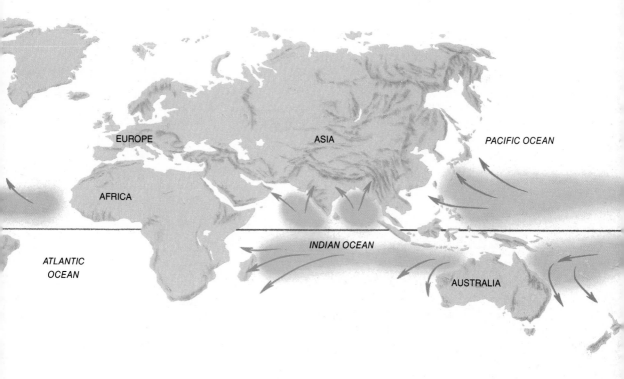

with winds of at least 74 miles an hour. Invariably the storms form over water and draw power from the oceanic heat source. After landfall, deprived of their heat, they weaken. Hurricanes occur most frequently in summer and fall when ocean temperatures peak. Because of its vast expanse the North Pacific Ocean has the most tropical cyclones each year, its western portion averaging about 26 during the season; most of them never make landfall. In contrast, no full-fledged hurricanes have ever been reported in the South Atlantic. That part of the ocean, some meteorologists speculate, is not large enough or warm enough to fuel such storms.

Hurricanes are among the most dramatic manifestations of nature's large-scale fury. One storm can have a diameter of about 700 miles, the distance between New York and Chicago, and may rise higher than 40,000 feet. As fearsome as they are, the storms, like the Maya creator-destroyer god, can be beneficial, bringing needed rainfall to areas parched by drought. More than 40 inches of rain have been measured in a hurricane. Even a storm of moderate force has produced rainfall equaling the average annual discharge of the Colorado River at its point of greatest flow. But picture this powerful engine of nature in its most destructive mode:

*T*he greatest natural disaster in United States history occurred on September 8, 1900, when a hurricane struck Galveston, Texas, and killed more than 6,000 people. Describing the catastrophe in the October 1900 NATIONAL GEOGRAPHIC, geologist W J McGee wrote: "The darkest horror of American history has fallen on our southern coast; a city comparable in population and wealth with Ephesus and Sodom of old, with Herculaneum and Pompeii of appalling memory, and with earthquake-wrecked Lisbon of later centuries, is blotted out in a night. Thirty-eight thousand people, the life and soul of a progressive and thriving city, are overwhelmed and doubly decimated by wind and wave in the darkness; literal thousands are crushed in their own falling houses or drowned in the raging waters; every survivor is made homeless, and most of them are utterly impoverished. The morning's sun rises on a scene of suffering and devastation hardly paralleled in the history of the world— a scene which has been, and will be again and again, described by tongue and pen, but never in more than a fraction or suggestion of the ghastly details."

Florida knew disaster in 1928, when wind-driven waters overflowed Lake Okeechobee; most of the 1,836 casualties had drowned. Ten years later 600 people died in a hurricane that battered Long Island and southern New England. Since 1953, women's names (and more recently men's as well) have been officially used by the National Weather Service to identify the storms. Hurricane Donna meandered from Florida to Maine in 1960, striking land and then veering out to sea, where it reintensified before striking again. This was the first storm with hurricane-force winds to wreak such a long path of destruction in 75 years of record keeping. In 1967 Hurricane Beulah generated 115 tornadoes in Texas. Agnes, in 1972, became one of the costliest natural disasters in U.S. history, causing some two billion dollars' worth of property damage. The number of hurricanes that hit the East and Gulf coasts in 1985, six in all, was the largest on record since 1916.

Yet the seasonal losses inflicted on the United States by these storms cannot compare with the death and destruction often caused by those that strike the Bay of Bengal and the Ganges Delta. In November 1970 at least 300,000 people perished in what is now Bangladesh as a tropical cyclone drove a wall of seawater with waves more than 22 feet high across low-lying islands. It is not uncommon for a single storm in the area to kill several thousand people. In 1985, for example, 10,000 died in Bangladesh during the annual reenactment of nature's devastating drama.

"The forces of nature are awesome compared with what we humans can do," Dr. Neil Frank, director of the National Hurricane Center, told me in his office in Coral Gables, Florida. He gestured emphatically, and his eyes widened at the scope of the subject. "Man has created a terrible problem in Bangladesh. It's like Louisiana if you put hundreds of thousands of people down where people don't even live in Louisiana. In Bangladesh the people who plant on those islands—they know the problems with cyclones, but they're willing to take the risks because the alternative is to starve. There's no other choice. It's a problem without a solution.

"But in the United States, it's the affluent who have found those same kinds of islands. Local governments have encouraged development on them. Many people who go out and buy there don't even know there's a risk. How many of us have experienced the *biggie?* Very few. A big hurricane is a rare event. The people I'm concerned about are those who have been on the fringe of a hurricane and think they know what it's all about. Out of 75 condominium buildings I've been in, only two had salespeople who knew of a hurricane problem. Blind leading the blind. Building codes depend on local governments, for the most part. Some Florida counties have rather stringent building codes, but many have minimal ones. Some buildings are designed to withstand 75-to-85-mile-an-hour winds. That's not a strong hurricane. I'm concerned about building death traps, and that's what I fear is happening.

"Nature is no respecter of economic status. People think, 'I went out there and paid a million dollars for my penthouse. Nothing can happen to that!' Well, you know, I'm *sorry* that you lost your yacht and your condo, but my first question is, 'Did you and your family get back to high ground? Are you safe?'

"I'm not against development, but there are so many people out on those islands that we probably won't be able to give enough lead time in some future warning to get them all to high ground."

Studies by many coastal towns and counties estimate time needed for evacuation, one of Dr. Frank's major concerns. "In 1980 in the coastal counties from Texas to Maine there were 40 million people," he said. "Probably the most frightening meteorological surprise that we worry about is when you have a weak hurricane approaching and then in the final hours, 12 to 20 before landfall, significant strengthening takes place and people don't have time to respond. For example, comprehensive evacuation studies now show us that it takes almost 30 hours to evacuate the Florida Keys. There'd be no way we'd get people out of the Keys if that kind of scenario developed. In 1935 a hurricane with winds probably in excess of 200 miles an hour pushed a dome of water 18 feet high right across the Keys. A rescue train was washed off the track. Some 400 people died.

"There are three things in a hurricane that we worry about," Dr. Frank continued. "First of all, everybody knows that hurricanes are big winds. The second thing you worry about is heavy rains. It's interesting, the amount of rainfall you get doesn't depend on how strong the winds are, but on how fast the system is moving. You can have a slow-moving storm and get 20 to 30 inches of rain. You can have a fast-moving, intense hurricane that might give you only five inches."

Flash floods can be one result of rains induced by hurricanes. Fifi, which hit Honduras in 1974, was not an awesome storm, Dr. Frank noted. "But it produced heavy rains in the mountains. Mud slides and debris made a natural dam along a river. The water built up behind it, finally burst it, and down came all this water and some 2,000 people died."

In October 1985 flash floods and mud slides killed a hundred people in Puerto Rico when huge amounts of rain fell from a turbulent mass of air that, days later, would become tropical storm Isabel. Isabel was followed by Juan, the costliest storm of the season, with damages estimated at more than 1.5 billion dollars. Though not a strong hurricane, Juan generated excessive rainfall and caused the worst flooding in decades along the Louisiana coast before making final landfall near Pensacola, Florida. As the remnants of Juan moved north over the Appalachian Mountains, they joined a persistent local storm. The mass hovered over parts of West Virginia, Virginia, Pennsylvania, and Maryland for nearly a week, dumping 18 inches of rain in one area. When major rivers rampaged out of their banks, 43 people died.

"The third thing," Dr. Frank continued, "the most awesome part of the hurricane from the standpoint of life, is the storm surge; the stronger the hurricane, the higher the dome. This dome of salt water may be 50 miles wide and can be 10, 20, and in the case of Camille in 1969, 25 feet high. Just visualize a dome of water 25 feet high, bring it across the coastline, then put 10-foot waves on top of it. If you have no elevation, like southern Louisiana, the dome will drop off one or two feet every mile it goes inland. Then if it hits at high tide—it's an awesome problem. If you have bays, if you have rivers, it can reach way back up into inland areas."

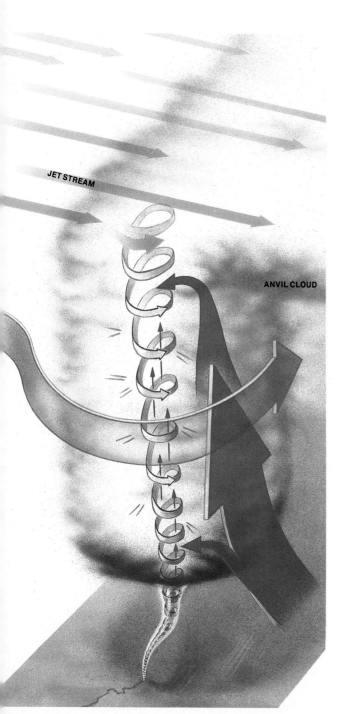

The most powerful tornadoes often take shape in a "supercell," a single giant thunderstorm. The southeastern portion, or right flank, of such a storm is shown here. Before the storm formed, strong winds from the west blew over weaker winds near the surface, creating a horizontal roll. Warm,

humid air from the south, colliding with the westerlies, rose and built the cloud, pushing the horizontal roll upward into the vertical spin seen here. At jet-stream heights the rising air fans out to form the anvil cloud, which may extend hundreds of miles. Like any vortex, the spinning updraft tends to draw in,

JET STREAM

ANVIL CLOUD

For all these reasons Hurricane Gloria became the most publicized tropical cyclone in history as it approached the East Coast in September 1985. Experts classified Gloria as extremely dangerous and warned accordingly. Living in a suburb of Washington, D.C., and alerted by news media (most often by Dr. Frank on television), my family and I stocked up on candles, flashlights, food, water, dry firewood, and a battery-powered radio. This time we awaited nature's huff and puff in a house made of bricks. But Gloria's center remained over water and the mid-Atlantic states were spared her extreme wrath. She moved over Long Island just at low tide with a storm surge of only seven feet and did minimal damage.

"Lucky! Oh, it's unreal!" said Dr. Frank, raising his hands in remembered relief. "At high tide there would have been five or six more feet of water with wave action on top of it. Islands would have been inundated."

Statistics show that between 1955 and 1975 at least 90 percent of hurricane deaths were caused by drowning. The storm surge of Camille, one of the strongest hurricanes on record, with gusts of 175 miles an hour over land, inundated the Mississippi coast with deep water and battered it with high waves. More than 125 people drowned.

Storm surge also caused the Galveston disaster of 1900; the city on its low-lying barrier island literally went underwater. "The makers of Galveston erred," wrote W J McGee, "in building their houses on the sands, in planting their city within reach of the waves, in domiciling their helpless ones on a sinking coast."

Dr. Frank explained problems associated with preventing such disasters. "There's a perception by the public that

we're doing a great job of forecasting. No!
We're doing a great job of *observing*. Hurricanes move along in rivers of air, just like
rivers of water on land. The difference is
that in the atmosphere there aren't any
riverbanks, and so the rivers of air move
around. We observe by satellite, weather
planes, radar, and sometimes ships, but
there are atmospheric measurements we
just don't have now. If we have 30 hours'
lead time and forecast a hurricane to go
right over a community, four out of five
times it goes someplace else. We'd have to
spend a lot more money to get better forecasts. Economically it's not feasible."

I wondered aloud to Dr. Frank why our
creator-destroyer, mother nature, chooses
to produce hurricanes—such machines of
swirling annihilation.

"Hurricanes are not freak acts of nature designed to inflict death and destruction on mankind," he explained. "They
perform a very useful function in the atmosphere. In a broad sense, we get too much
heat in the tropics and not enough heat in
the polar latitudes because of the way the
sun shines on the globe, and we've got to do
something to mix up the warm and cold air
or it becomes intolerable to live. Winter
storms are the primary way this mixing
takes place most of the year—they're like
giant eggbeaters. Because we continue to
gain heat in the tropics and lose heat in polar latitudes, we've got to have a lot of these
eggbeaters. Their basic purpose is to move
cold air to regions of warm air and warm
air to cold regions. All weather systems are
designed to move heat around.

"Now, in the summer the boundary
between cold and warm air moves back
north. The tropics begin to boil, get heat
and heat and more heat, and you've got to
get rid of that heat. Nature has a very effective way of doing it, and it's called the hurricane. In a sense the hurricane represents
the tropical atmosphere boiling. If we
didn't have this unequal distribution of
heat on the planet, we wouldn't have to
have weather systems."

If few have experienced the "biggie"—
a hurricane of extreme force—most
have witnessed another spectacular phenomenon, the thunderstorm. Who has not
paused at the sound of distant rumbling or
felt the rush of cool air as a summer storm
approached? Or winced at the sight of jagged lightning or felt a thunderclap reverberate like the very pulse of the universe?

The first such roiling spectacle on record may be one in Babylonia described by
the Prophet Ezekiel more than 2,500 years
ago: "And I looked, and, behold, a whirlwind came out of the north, a great cloud,
and a fire infolding itself, and a brightness
was about it, and out of the midst thereof
as the colour of amber, out of the midst of
the fire." Ezekiel likened the storm to the
glory of God.

This thrilling show of nature's force is
a frequent one: About 2,000 thunderstorms
are in progress over the earth's surface at
any given moment. Some 45,000 form daily
and 16 million annually around the world.
They are far more common in some areas
than in others; Java provides an extreme
example, with an average of 223 days of
thunder each year. Central Florida experiences the most thunderstorm days in the
United States, about 90 annually. Thunderstorms are rare in Washington State and
Oregon, areas of relatively high rainfall,
but prone to long, quiet rains rather than
noisy displays and sudden cloudbursts.

If an entire storm system is an eggbeater, a thunderstorm is a whisk, turning over layers of warm and cold air in a relatively small area. It is a towering cumulonimbus cloud that acts like a hot-air balloon, beginning with updrafts of warm air and expanding as water vapor changes to liquid or frozen particles, thereby releasing heat. This heat expands the cloud-balloon to its fullest capacity, and the mature cloud, or thunderstorm, may measure several miles across at its base and rise to an altitude of 40,000 feet or more.

These local, or convective, storms form independently and last an hour or two before dissipating. There are also two other types. Organized thunderstorms, which occur along weather fronts, can be violent, often last for hours, and may produce lightning, hail, heavy rainfall and flash floods, winds of 60 miles an hour or more, and, at times, tornadoes. In recent years scientists have identified a third type, which they call a mesoscale convective complex—a group of thunderstorms that spawn still more thunderstorms and support a widespread region of rainfall. They occur most frequently at night. Discovered through satellite imagery, these systems often assume a circular shape with a wide, clear center. They can be a thousand times larger than an individual storm and spread across six or more states.

Whatever its type and size, to be classified as severe a thunderstorm must meet certain criteria. According to Don Burgess of the National Severe Storms Laboratory in Norman, Oklahoma, it must produce hail at least three-fourths of an inch in diameter, have winds of more than 50 miles an hour, and spawn at least one tornado.

Although a severe storm can be a blessing with its rain and cooling temperatures, mankind dreads the destructive violence that may accompany it. Strong winds, heavy rains, hail, lightning, and tornadoes—these are the "children of the storm." And our attention is fixed most of all on the sudden and terrifying tornado.

On land they are called tornadoes, twisters, whirlwinds, or cyclones; at sea and on lakes they are known as waterspouts. By any name they are the most violent of all storms. "A tornado," an Oklahoma wag explained to me, "is a storm that plucks a flock of chickens clean and turns rabbits wrong side out." Scientists offer a more prosaic definition: a violently rotating column of air that descends from a thunderstorm cloud system. Tornadoes form within rotating thunderstorms when the jet stream is overhead and strong winds are aloft.

"If you had a giant board," Don Burgess explained, "and I'm talking about a really long one maybe a couple of thousand feet long, and you stuck it up in the sky, it would begin to turn on a horizontal axis like a whirling propeller or a paddle wheel, because winds are stronger aloft than near the ground. You also get a strong updraft that comes with a thunderstorm. The updraft tilts the board so that it begins whirling on a vertical axis at high speed like a skater pulling her arms in and spinning. It spins faster and faster in a small diameter until you get this violent whirlwind."

A tornado may stretch upward to the top of a towering thunderstorm; it brings death and destruction when it reaches down to touch the earth. Argentina, Australia, England, the Soviet Union, and India are among the countries that experience tornadoes, but more form in the United States than in any other place on earth; between 700 and a thousand are reported each year. While they occur in every state, Texas holds the record with an annual average of 120. That state lies at the southern end of "Tornado Alley," where tornadoes strike most often, an area stretching from north-central Texas through Oklahoma into eastern Kansas. The combination of dry, potentially cold westerly winds from the Rocky Mountains, moisture from the Gulf of Mexico, and the flat topography of the plains creates ideal conditions for thunderstorms to form—and then to give birth to this violent child.

Tornadoes vary widely in aspect and behavior. Rate of travel can range from a dawdling pace to about 70 miles an hour. Size can range from a twister a few feet wide, dangling harmlessly above the landscape like a jittery rope, to a lethal, mile-wide funnel leveling everything in its path.

The worst tornadoes leave appalling statistics in their wake. The record for distance and duration was set in May 1917, when a tornado cut a path 293 miles long from Missouri into Indiana in more than seven hours. The deadliest was the tri-state tornado of 1925, which killed 689 people as it swept Missouri, Illinois, and Indiana. The greatest number of storms developed on April 3 and 4, 1974, when more than 140 twisters caused 315 deaths, 5,500 injuries, and half a billion dollars' worth of property damage from Alabama to Ohio.

Eyewitness accounts of tornadoes have provided some of the most dramatic descriptions of nature on the rampage. In 1794 a Connecticut newspaper gave this report of a twister in New Milford: "It passed like a high and extensive flood of darkness, tumbling and curling with the most rapid motion, in the wildest confusion, full of branches of trees, boards, doors, casks, cloths, wool, and some think they saw animals of various kinds, it is certain, many geese, fowls, &c. are missing where it passed in this town, and cannot be found. One thing deserves particular notice for its sublimity; it was a Tamarac tree which had been taken up by the roots, and was carried along in the position it grew. Sometimes it would settle down almost to the ground, then rise with rapidity 300 feet in the air: thus it danced along till it went out of the view of the astonished spectators, and what heightened the sublimity, 2 or 3 large objects, supposed to be barn-doors, appeared to play with the tree, attending around it in all its vagaries."

Such spectacular facts have been adapted to fiction: Dorothy and her dog, Toto, rose into a twister's vortex and flew past familiar objects and a bicycling neighborhood busybody before being deposited in Oz. But real survivors' stories are equally bizarre: A man who was drawn up into a tornado in Wichita Falls, Texas, claimed that while aloft he saw a house trailer pass by with a woman inside standing at a window. He recalled longing to reach a mattress flying ahead so that he could rest; then he lost consciousness and awoke on the ground tangled in barbed wire. Like Dorothy, a Kansas woman was spun up into the air and whirled in a vortex. She finally landed beside a phonograph record. Its title: "Stormy Weather."

Few people have dealt directly with tornadoes, but Benjamin Franklin got close to what might have been a small one. In 1755, on a visit to Maryland, he rode horseback near what he called a whirlwind. He later wrote: "As it is a common opinion that a shot, fired through a water-spout, will break it, I tried to break this little whirlwind, by striking my whip frequently through it, but without any effect."

Now, more than 200 years later, students of storms still dream of ridding the world of twisters.

"We're way too ignorant still," said Don Burgess. "Once the tornado's formed we'd have to expend too much energy to dissipate it. For instance, a nuclear device would release a comparable amount of energy. That would dissipate the tornado all right, but it would do tremendous damage of its own. We might create a dozen tornadoes if we interacted incorrectly. Knowledge and care would be essential. It may be 50 years or more before we interact with a storm so that all that energy doesn't get concentrated in the first place."

Burgess and his stalwart colleagues, however, do chase thunderstorms that could produce tornadoes. If their mechanical TOTO is ever inside a funnel, it will yield valuable information. TOTO, short for Totable Tornado Observatory, is a sealed cylinder bristling with antennas and filled with instruments. Each year from April into June research teams chase promising thunderstorms in Tornado Alley, racing to place TOTO in the path of a twister. So far success has been limited.

"When it happens, we'll get fantastic data," says Burgess. "We'll get more information about wind, atmospheric pressure, temperature, and moisture. We want to know in detail about the workings of a tornado: For instance, what is the relationship between wind and pressure? Is there a secondary vortex?"

Tornado researchers strive to prevent

tragedy. "We use a combination of radar and trained spotters to issue warnings," Burgess explained. "The radars we have don't identify tornadoes particularly well. Spotters have the greatest accuracy. Unfortunately, the tornado the spotter reports is already forming or has touched the ground before a warning goes out. The average warning time is short, probably less than five minutes, perhaps only two or three. By 1990 a nationwide system of Doppler radars will give better warnings."

The radars are named after Christian J. Doppler, an Austrian physicist who in the 1840s became the first person to realize that the frequency of sound waves increases or decreases depending upon whether the wave source and the observer are moving toward or away from each other. Further, the changes in frequency could be measured. The same principle applies to electromagnetic waves, so that astronomers can determine the relative velocities of stars and their distance from the earth and meteorologists can measure the behavior of winds inside clouds.

"With Doppler we can see the wind velocity, the rotation up inside the storm," Burgess said. "We can't see that with conventional radar. We think we will have a longer lead time—up to 20 minutes before the funnel can do damage."

In simple terms, he explained, "a tornado's just a spin-up, an eddy. We have eddies all the time up in the clouds, like swirls in creeks and in dust devils. They are a manifestation of flow, an energy distribution mechanism."

For a moment he mused more as an observer than a scientist. "Tornadoes are so awesome because they are such magnificent concentrations of energy in a narrow area, powerful things with winds maybe approaching 250 miles an hour or more. They're tall, they're big. You have sensory overload when you see one. Anything man-made pales in comparison."

One man-made creation, the airplane, is especially vulnerable to the violent power concentrated in another child of the storm. This recently discovered offspring is a type of wind shear—a change of wind speed or

direction or both over a short distance. Called a downburst or microburst, the type has been known to us only since 1976. Dr. T. Theodore Fujita of the University of Chicago deduced the existence of microbursts after helping investigate the crash of an Eastern Airlines Boeing 727 in 1975 as it made a final approach to Kennedy International Airport in New York City. He found that the plane had encountered an intense head-wind-to-tail-wind shift in wind direction. His discovery later explained the 1982 crash of a Pan American World Airways jet soon after takeoff from New Orleans and several other puzzling accidents of previous years. From 1964 through August 1985, more than 600 people died and at least 235 were injured in such crashes.

Today scientists know that microburst wind shears are intense concentrations of sinking air that usually form along the leading edges of thunderstorms ahead of shafts of rain. But many are the "dry" type associated with evaporated rain shafts that can render them almost invisible. A microburst has been called an "upside-down tornado." The column of air behaves somewhat like pancake batter poured onto a hot griddle. When the rapidly sinking air approaches the ground, it spreads out from the center in all directions. A plane flying into a microburst encounters strong head winds and increasing lift, and the pilot may try to compensate by leveling off. Then as the plane flies through the microburst it is suddenly hit by a powerful downdraft and tail wind.

Dr. J. Murray Mitchell, senior research climatologist with the National Oceanic and Atmospheric Administration (NOAA), explained the phenomenon to me. With his outspread hand he imitated an airplane flying out of a microburst. "You suddenly find yourself in air that's moving slower in relation to you, making you lose more lift on the wings." His hand sank ominously toward his desk. "If you're too close to the ground at that point, there's no way out. You'll crash."

Thunderstorms that form microbursts usually create several successive ones of various strengths and sizes. At times they create tornadoes as well. The wind speeds in microbursts can equal those in strong tornadoes and even produce the same roaring sound as twisters. NOAA warns: "The occurrence of downbursts makes it imperative that the threat of severe thunderstorms be taken as seriously as that of tornadoes." Airlines increasingly do just that, training pilots to deal with such hazardous conditions, and keeping in mind that in the United States alone an estimated 3,510 potentially damaging microbursts occur each year—about four times the average number of tornadoes.

Perhaps the least understood child of the storm is one of the earliest on record. Some seven or eight centuries before Ezekiel described the whirling thunderstorm, hail became one of the plagues that devastated Egypt: "And Moses stretched forth his rod toward heaven: and the Lord sent thunder and hail, and the fire ran along upon the ground; and the Lord rained hail upon the land of Egypt." Lightning and hail, fire and ice, they came as divine punishment. The Book of Exodus relates that the hail ruined flax and barley ready for harvest and pummeled man and beast. Hail is common throughout the temperate regions of the world, and mankind is no less helpless today against its onslaught.

In the United States the thunderstorm-produced phenomenon occurs so often where Colorado, Nebraska, and Wyoming meet that the area is called "Hail Alley"; hailstorms occur there ten or more days a year. Hail also falls frequently on the plains and along the northern Pacific coast.

Hailstones form as colliding drops of moisture freeze together in the cold upper regions of a thunderstorm. As the aggregate falls, it collects more freezing moisture. Strong updrafts may lift it repeatedly so that more layers of ice form around it before it finally falls to earth. A large hailstone may have ten or more layers. Hailstones can be round, oval, or pear-shaped, or as knobbed and dimpled as a potato; they can be as small as peas or as large as grapefruit. The largest weigh between one and two pounds and fall at about a hundred miles an hour. The results may vary from a few scattered hailstones to an accumulation three feet deep.

Since spring and summer are the likeliest seasons for hail, damage to high-value crops is costly—averaging about 700 million dollars each year in the United States alone. Hailstorms may be less visually dramatic than tornadoes, but they can be more destructive of life. In September 1985 one storm in Brazil killed at least 22 people and injured a thousand, most of them in houses that collapsed beneath the weight of the hail. A slow-moving August storm, said to be the worst in memory, struck Cheyenne, Wyoming, in 1985 and dumped six inches of rain and six inches of hail in less than four hours; 12 people perished in the storm and ensuing flash flood.

Hail is also more difficult to predict than tornadoes. Most thunderstorms probably produce hailstones, but in only a few do they survive to reach the ground. In experiments to suppress hail formation, Americans have fired rockets from aircraft and Russians have shot artillery shells into clouds. Both have attempted to seed likely hail-producing storms with silver iodide, reasoning that its particles would inhibit formation of large stones. The results are inconclusive. Until research leads to practical solutions, hail will remain the most erratic and obstreperous child of the storm.

*H*uman encounters with the forces of nature have given rise to beliefs and customs passed down through generations. Maya farmers of Yucatán still offer gifts to Chaac, ancient god of rain, thunder, and lightning, and implore him to send seasonal moisture for their crops. They believe he and lesser Chaacs gather as rain clouds and ride across the sky on horseback. One makes thunderclaps that sound like the cracks of a whip. Each pours rain from a gourd with one hand and in the other brandishes a long machete-like blade that creates lightning.

Yucatán is a flat land, and from a lofty structure you can see for miles. I have known the heat to build and the Chaac-clouds to gather at night along a horizon so distant there is no sound of the thunder whip, nor are you even aware of the storms until the lightning-blades illuminate the massive clouds with fire from within. Swords of light flash inside each cloud only to disappear. Blackness returns. Suddenly the swords streak down to touch the earth, then cross, repel, attract each other in mid-air, glow within the clouds once more, then desist, only to begin again. It is an ever changing spectacle. It is like witnessing creation itself.

Scientists believe such majestic displays may have marked our beginning. In his book *Understanding Lightning*, Dr. Martin A. Uman of the University of Florida at Gainesville pondered the possibility, suggested by others before him, that "it may well have been lightning in the primordial soup covering the earth several billion years ago that produced the complex molecules from which life eventually evolved. . . . Thus, we may be indebted to lightning for the presence of life on earth."

For thousands of years mankind associated lightning with divine punishment. Then the Greek philosopher Aristotle, in the fourth century B.C., proposed that lightning was burning wind. More than 20 centuries later, in 1752, Benjamin Franklin flew his famous kite during a thunderstorm; his dangerous experiment proved that lightning is electrical. He had reasoned that clouds are electrically charged. To verify this, he attached a wire to a kite frame and sent the kite aloft. After a long wait, he felt an electric spark course through his hand from a metal key fastened to the end of the kite string. Later, people began putting metal rods on buildings to conduct lightning harmlessly to the ground.

Lightning remains a universal concern. From the 2,000 thunderstorms in progress above the earth's surface at any given time, about a hundred cloud-to-ground lightning discharges occur each second—more than eight million every day. In the United States lightning ignites some 2,000 rural structures and starts 10,000 forest fires each year. Between 1970 and 1984, it killed 1,154 people here; during the same period 1,341 perished in hurricanes and tornadoes combined.

Normally the earth is negatively charged. Within a thunderstorm, an intense electrical field develops, with negative charges in the lower part of the cloud and positive charges in the upper part. The negative charge in the cloud induces a positive charge on the ground for several miles around the storm. Lightning occurs when the charges become strong enough to overcome resistance in insulating air and a current flows between the two charges. Thus, lightning can leap from negative to positive charges within a cloud, from cloud to ground, or from elevated objects on the ground to a cloud.

The lightning we see is a bright channel of high temperature more than four times hotter than the surface of the sun, or about 50,000°F. Channels longer than 90 miles have been observed, but the average measures three or four miles. A 100-watt light bulb uses about one ampere of electrical current; lightning currents can range up to hundreds of thousands of amps.

"There's been one-third as much lightning research done since about 1970 as in all of recorded history before then," Dr. Uman told me. "We have gathered a lot of detailed information not available before. Now we know more precisely where the charges are in the clouds. The negative charge is distributed more or less horizontally, whereas previously we thought it was a more or less vertical column. The positive

Microburst wind shear, an intense downflow of air that spatters as it hits ground, presents extreme danger to aircraft landing or taking off. The microburst may whoosh out of a low thunderstorm—or out of an evaporated rain shaft, so that the path seems clear. Taking off into a microburst, the plane meets

charge is scattered over the top of the cloud in a diffuse way. Other new findings relate to the characteristics of currents. They are faster than we thought, rising to peak value in tenths of a microsecond. That has a lot of implications for lightning protection.

"Lightning location systems that detect magnetic fields radiated by lightning have been developed over the past several years," he continued. "Now, over more than two-thirds of North America, systems plot lightning on TV-screen maps within a second after it strikes the ground. Kennedy Space Center has a system it uses for launches. Similar systems are used for forest fire warnings, by power companies, by meteorologists for storm warnings, by the Federal Aviation Administration for airplanes. It's amazing how it's caught on—from basic research in the early '70s to this essentially complete use." Dr. Uman and Dr. E. P. Krider of the University of Arizona were the primary developers.

Technology has given us astounding aids to help mitigate hurricane and thunderstorm hazards: weather satellites, Doppler radar, lightning location and protection systems—and TOTO, too. While amazing abilities to avert disaster lie at our fingertips, safety through technology alone is far from assured. The human factor remains vital.

A concerned Neil Frank had told me, "If you go to California and build your house on a fault line, *don't fuss* about earthquakes. And if you go to the Carolinas, or the Jersey coast, or the Texas or Florida coast and build on one of these little islands offshore, *don't fuss* about hurricanes." He reflected a moment, then added quietly, "If human beings would live in harmony with the forces of nature, we could minimize our problems."

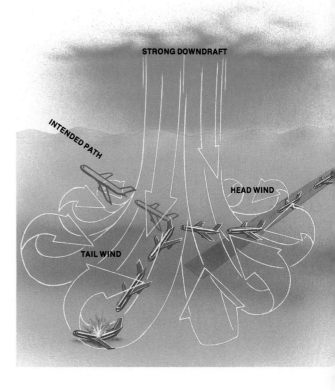

STRONG DOWNDRAFT

INTENDED PATH

HEAD WIND

TAIL WIND

a wind shear, a strong head wind; airspeed increases, a boon for the climb out. Then comes another shear, and another, as within a mile or two the craft enters the downdraft and the opposite flow. In the strong tail wind, airspeed drops and may approach the verge of a stall—as the aircraft fights for altitude.

FOLLOWING PAGES: Hurricane Allen flails Corpus Christi, Texas, in August 1980. With churning winds of 190 miles an hour, it left 250 dead in the Caribbean. Though the giant storm filled the Gulf of Mexico and dropped 16 inches of rain on Texas, it lost much of its lethal power before striking the coast.

From storm center to nerve center, reports and images flow in, building a running profile of a hurricane. Meteorologists in Coral Gables, Florida (below), read the omens on video monitors, compute the storm's power and progress, and spread the word—which may help millions to keep out of harm's way, from the Caribbean to the Gulf coast to New England. Satellite images taken at 23,000 miles above the Equator locate the storm and present a broad picture of its strength. The patterns opposite, color enhanced for clearer contrast, show variations in cloud intensity; dark cores may indicate heavy rains and severe winds. The lower image pinpoints the hurricane eye between Cuba and the Yucatán Peninsula. At right, the flight meteorologist (left foreground, behind the flight engineer and pilots) obtains readings of rainfall, wind strength, and atmospheric pressure in and around the eye—a key indicator of severity. When the hurricane is 24 hours from land, Orion aircraft provide continuous coverage of its track and vital signs.

ALL, PAUL CHESLEY

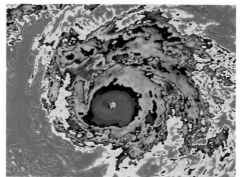

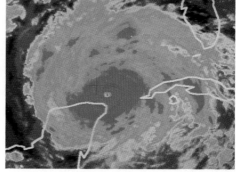

ALL, PAUL CHESLEY

136

Keeping a worried eye on islands in the storm zones, Neil Frank, director of the National Hurricane Center, sees potential death traps in densely developed barrier beaches with few escape routes. Above the Florida coast (left) the picture comes into perspective—high-rise resorts whose occupants must funnel across bridges to the mainland. State-of-the-art forecasting provides, at best, 12 hours' warning of a hurricane's landfall; some coastal areas need more than a day to evacuate. At Dauphin Island, near Mobile, Alabama, Frank (below) surveys the impact of Hurricane Elena on Labor Day weekend, 1985. Winds of 122 miles an hour crumpled one beach house, turned another into a breezeway. Deputy Sheriff John Mitchell noted that tie-downs—inch-wide metal strips nailed from roof to pilings—helped island homes stand up to Elena. Though insured losses in four states came to 543 million dollars, few lives were lost. Timely warnings meshed with evacuation plans to put 1.5 million people on the move, perhaps the most massive evacuation in U.S. history. When Camille ripped the Mississippi coast in 1969, 149 died; the toll led to major changes in emergency procedures.

"... and the windows of heaven were stopped ... the waters returned from off the earth...." As in Genesis, so in the autumn of 1985, after the remnants of Hurricane Juan brought West Virginia the worst floods in its history. Evelyn Hendrickson leafs through a family Bible while her husband, Henry, inspects the living room—ruined when the South Branch of the Potomac River invaded their Petersburg home. In Rowlesburg the house that George Lee built floated away with the Cheat River. "Where can I begin at 77 years of age?" he asked. In time a modular home replaced the work of his hands.

FOLLOWING PAGES: *Patroling National Guardsmen take soundings at 17th and Main as the muddy James flows gently through the capital of Virginia. Richmond's old Shockoe Bottom district lay under as much as 12 feet of water when the flood of 1985 crested and rolled on to the sea.*

BOB SACHA (ABOVE); STEVE WALL (OPPOSITE); SAM ABELL (FOLLOWING PAGES)

Busiest airport in the world, Chicago's O'Hare averages more than 2,200 operations every weekday. In ideal weather, with six runways in use, the tower controllers handle as many as 110 landings and 75 takeoffs an hour. Foggy or storm-fouled skies can cut the capacity by a third or more. Three radars sweep a 20-mile radius, displaying each plane's ID, speed, and altitude. Above the scope on the right flash the wind readings of the Low-Level Wind Shear Alert System; it can warn of sharp variations at the field perimeter but cannot reliably detect the ultrahazardous shear known as microburst.

FOLLOWING PAGES: *Charred hulk of Delta 191 lies at Dallas-Fort Worth, felled in a rainsquall in August 1985, killing 137. "It seemed like there was something . . . pushing it to the ground," said a survivor. The craft's loss of airspeed—60 knots in 17 seconds— points to microburst wind shears.*

New skills, new tools enter the pilot's high-tech world to help him elude, or survive, a microburst wind shear. At the American Airlines Flight Academy in Fort Worth, trainees confront simulated air turbulence controlled by the instructor behind them. "To maintain the desired flight path in a

microburst," says director Bill James, "the pilot may have to let the airspeed decay below what he would ever normally see on his indicator." Near Seattle a Boeing simulation (left) displays a microburst pattern: Winds shoot down in the center, then curl outward and around. Production line (opposite) includes 737-300s, first Boeing type to get technology designed to identify wind shear, sound an alert, and chart a safe response. Airborne Doppler radar units—offering advance warning of a microburst and thus enabling pilots to avoid it—lie in the future.

147

*A midsummer nightmare struck Cheyenne,
the city's worst single-day storm on record.
"It was like someone opened a faucet
immediately above Cheyenne and set it on
superhigh velocity," declared Mayor Don
Erickson. Six inches of rain—half the average
annual precipitation—fell in less than four*

hours. Jackie Jensen and her husband, Jan (above), took to their attic, prepared to kick out a wall if the rising waters threatened them. Cold light of day brought little comfort; nearly flooded out, the Jensens were now frozen in. The downpour had swept six inches of hail into drifts as deep as eight feet. Creeks ran wild, flooding cars, drowning occupants. Twelve died. Canoes took to some streets, snowplows to others. "The kind of storm we had is a once-in-a-100-or-200-year thing," observed a weatherman. August 1, 1985, toppled a Cheyenne record set 89 years earlier—4.7 inches of hail on July 15, 1896.

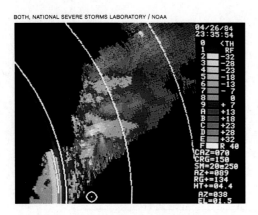

A glowering thundercloud with no rainfall beneath it . . . spinning droplets of rain spotted by radar 70 miles away. To seasoned eyes, and to the marvel of Doppler radar, budding tornadoes reveal telltale signs well before the deadly funnel forms. Several clues stand out in the storm cloud flaring over northern Texas, in notorious Tornado Alley. Spotters note the "rain-free base," the result of a strong updraft that keeps rain suspended within the cloud. The major surge of warm, moist air feeds into the churning mass at the "main storm tower," located directly above the nearest pole. The most riveting detail, however, looms just left of the pole; a slight upward bulge marks the "wall cloud"—the area of swiftest rotation and likeliest spot for a funnel. And there, minutes after the photograph was taken on April 10, 1979, a twister spun out, lacerating open fields near Seymour. An hour later and 50 miles to the northeast, the storm spawned another tornado. This one, a mile wide at the ground and with winds revving up to 225 miles an hour, tore through Wichita Falls, leveling 2,000 homes. Doppler radar bears the name of an Austrian physicist who died long before radar was born. But the phenomenon Christian Doppler described in the 1840s enables meteorologists today to "see" the inner workings of a storm. Sound waves, noted Doppler, change frequency as their source moves toward or away from the observer. Doppler radar (above) clocks the movement of rain droplets in a cloud. Range rings mark off 60, 80, and 100 miles from the radar at the National Severe Storms Laboratory in Norman, Oklahoma. Droplets moving toward the lab appear in green, the brightest hue indicating the highest speed, 32 meters (105 feet) a second. Brightest red indicates the same speed in the opposite direction. Where the brightest tones touch, some 70 miles out, droplets swirl to and fro at maximum speed—evidence of a strong spin. Seeing this just before midnight on April 26, 1984, NSSL observers tried to contact local officials. But an earlier storm had knocked out phone lines, aborting a relay to the danger zone. The tornado struck Morris, Oklahoma, without warning. Conventional radars can spot storms and gauge their intensity but cannot track their internal churnings. In 1986 only three Doppler weather radars were in operational use across the U.S. The heralded NEXRAD (Next Generation of Weather Radar) program plans to deploy 125 of them by 1990.

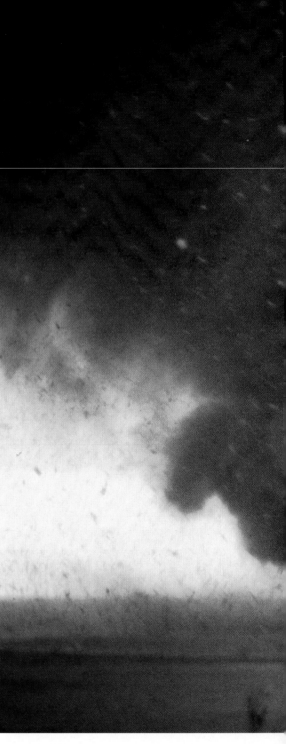

Like winnowed chaff, the Shannon Heights Trailer Park flies in the whirlwind as the most devastating tornado in Wyoming history rips through Cheyenne on July 16, 1979. Seventeen trailer homes—seven of them cinched with chain or cable tie-downs—went up in shreds. Nearby, at his home in northeastern Cheyenne, photographer Peter Willing saw the aerial maelstrom coming. When it drew to about 3,300 feet (upper left), he ducked into the basement. Then, deciding to chance it, he emerged to record the obliteration of the trailer park (left and above) 1,300 feet away. Suction extends

hundreds of feet beyond the vortex, the surge
of debris so thick that the very earth seems to
rise. Based on severity of damage, the twister
ranks just below the most violent. Wyoming
rarely sees this kind, for the High Plains
receive relatively little muggy air, the high-
octane fuel for tornadoes.

A swift-moving caldron of low pressure—
mixing hot, moist air from the Gulf of Mexico
and cold, dry air from Canada—exploded on
May 31, 1985, into the deadliest tornado
outbreak in more than a decade. Between
3 and 11 p.m., 43 tornadoes scarred Ohio,
Pennsylvania, New York, and southern

Ontario, taking 87 lives. Ten ranked as
"maxis"—the most violent—with one
whipping around at perhaps 300 miles an
hour. At Albion, Pennsylvania (left), a maxi
paused in the southwest part of town (lower
right corner), then carved a trail of ruin to the
northeast. At Barrie, Ontario (above and
right), another crumpled houses and cars,
and bent roof metal around trees. At Niles,
Ohio, 75,000-pound oil tanks caromed off
their pads. In Newton Falls, Ohio, a twister
picked up Mrs. Jewell Sponaugle. "The winds
would suck me up and then slap me back
down just like I was crepe paper," she
recalled. "The whole time it sounded like a
thousand freight trains inside my
head.... Then I realized that I was choking
because I had been pelted with so much mud
and gravel and glass.... As soon as I got my
eyes cleared out, I was able to look
out ... that's the first time I saw the tornado
funnel. It was sucking up Alan's Drug Store."

Bolts out of the black make heaven and earth luminous on stormy summer nights. Branched lightning with a bright main channel strikes the Tucson Mountains in Arizona (below). Night retreats and the Tucson skyline dims as a river of fire sizzles to earth, highlighting the thundercloud that sparked it (right). When lightning touches down, it sends forth electromagnetic energy across all frequencies —light waves we can see, radio waves we hear as static. Lightning direction finders tune in, locating each hit by triangulation; the data serve forecasters, air traffic managers, and power company repair crews. Even as the tornadoes of May 1985 raged, the detection center in Albany, New York, plotted a rapid sequence of strikes tracking eastward (left). Red and yellow dots show the plot for two three-hour periods; circles scribe 250-mile ranges from the direction finders. Researchers counted 19,735 flashes for the six hours and 62,000 over a 20-hour span—nearly one every second.

FOLLOWING PAGES: While the lights of Tucson blur in a 30-second time exposure, lightning dances across the mountains and sunset paints the cloud tops.

SUNY-Albany Lightning Detection Network

19735   05/31/85 23:10 - 06/01/85 05:10

TOM IVES (ABOVE, OPPOSITE, AND FOLLOWING PAGES)

Plagues, Pests, and People

by Tom Melham

"For they covered
the face of the whole earth,
so that the land
was darkened;
and they did eat
every herb of the land,
and all
the fruit of the trees...."

—*Exodus 10:15*

They are nature's blitzkrieg army: Absolutely fearless, never considering retreat, equally at ease in the air or on the ground, they wage their lightning wars by banding together in the millions, suddenly attacking and overrunning one area, then swiftly moving on to another. They have no use for sophisticated strategies or cumbersome supply lines; they simply ride prevailing breezes and live entirely off those lands they invade. Nor do they have any generals, for their rank-and-file masses merely take turns leading themselves. Those in front at any given moment soon alight and feed, while their immediate followers fly on a bit before landing; the process continues as others even farther back temporarily assume the lead only to relinquish it later. Eventually the rear guard's arrival overhead signals the original leaders to rise up and rejoin. And so these pillagers descend upon a landscape and roll over it like a giant tank tread, taking only minutes to denude acres. The greater their numbers become, the faster they travel, hopscotching sometimes for thousands of miles.

They are one of man's oldest and costliest enemies; mere mention of their name still conjures chilling visions of dense, living blizzards blotting out the sun, of multitudes falling to earth and streaming from horizon to horizon, leaving a wake of ravaged crops, leafless and barked trees, and famine. Little wonder that these beasts were featured in Exodus as one of the ten devastating punishments God inflicted upon Egypt's intransigent Pharaoh more than 3,000 years ago. They are, of course, locusts in plague.

Just what *is* a plague? Simply put, too much of a bad thing. Science translates it as a complex and often fascinating outbreak: The population of a particular species suddenly erupts, forcefully impinging upon other creatures as well as its surroundings. Plagues can be cyclical, fading away almost as abruptly as they arrive. Often their specific causes and mechanisms remain obscure for centuries, generating persistent myths, mystery, and fear. Yet while plague populations may surge to abnormal and terrifying levels, plagues themselves are perfectly natural, like volcanoes that alternate between dormancy and explosive activity. They represent, in fact, one form of nature's most striking rampages: its biological ones.

Consider the desert locust, one of 7,000 species of grasshopper to inhabit the world. It has plagued every civilization of Egypt, the Fertile Crescent, and the Indus Valley, and others besides. At Nineveh, Assyrian artists of the eighth century B.C. depicted these insects in bas-relief. So did the tomb carvers of Saqqara in Lower Egypt—many centuries before the events recorded in Exodus. Certainly, locusts were happily scorching the earth long before man arrived. But the coming of civilization—and agriculture—increased their food supply. Their sudden blooms and collapses of population defeated not only man's attempts to control them but also his powers of comprehension. Where did these insatiable robbers come from? Where did they go?

The locust's most remarkable trait always has been its ability to show up in huge numbers and then vanish. Throughout its current range—from Mauritania in northwestern Africa, across the Middle East to India and Bangladesh—questions as to why locust populations come and go so dramatically have traditionally elicited shrugs and talk of divine will. People of the Arab world have referred to the swarming insects as the "Army of Allah."

Their near-magical appearances and disappearances, however, do not stem from a divine sleight of hand, but have a biological explanation. In 1921, Russian-born entomologist Boris Uvarov discovered that this boom-and-bust insect never completely departs its generally arid range; instead, it alternates between a solitary and a gregarious phase. The former, relatively quiet, usually prevails. But occasionally soaking rains trigger the hatching of millions of locust eggs and the rapid growth of plant life that will sustain this population explosion. Solitary locusts are normally green and inconspicuous. But once the insects become crowded, they undergo certain behavioral and physical changes. They begin to aggregate and to take on much brighter markings of red, black, and yellow. Small groups quickly coalesce into ever larger and increasingly mobile bands. Given the right sequence of rainy periods over time and distance, as well as accompanying blooms of vegetation to feed upon, desert locusts may take only a few years to swell their numbers a thousandfold. Thus do plagues begin.

Before they end, tremendous agricultural and economic damage can result. The widespread locust plague of 1958 destroyed an estimated 167,000 tons of grain in Ethiopia alone—enough to feed a million people for a year. Another plague a decade later threatened crops throughout the Afro-Asian locust belt, which includes a fifth of the world's agricultural lands—and some of its poorest nations.

Fortunately, desert locusts do not infest other continents. But every region has its own plague creatures, which periodically recur. North America, for example, suffers damaging cycles of pinebark beetles, spruce budworms, and grasshoppers.

Crisscrossing continents and oceans, pandemics—epidemics of unusual extent and severity—comprise some of nature's most devastating biological rampages. And bubonic plague ranks as one of history's greatest scourges. Named for its painful buboes, or lymph-gland swellings, it

probably originated in Central Asia. Three pandemics have punctuated the past 1,500 years, the first (red arrows) reaching out from Egypt in the sixth century to engulf the Byzantine Empire and most of the known western world. The second (orange) began in the 1300s and invaded India, China, and

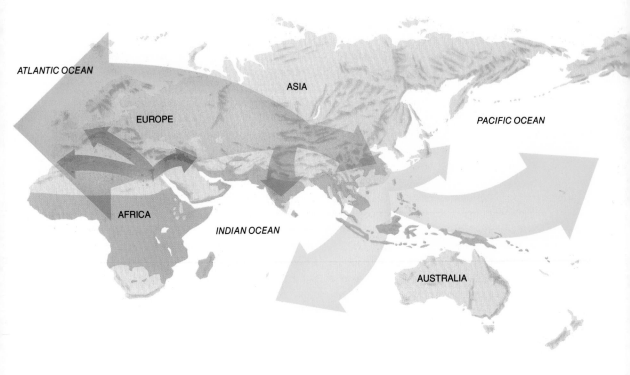

ATLANTIC OCEAN

ASIA

EUROPE

PACIFIC OCEAN

AFRICA

INDIAN OCEAN

AUSTRALIA

Some 700 grasshopper species abound in the United States alone, most posing no significant economic threat. One that does, however, is the so-called Mormon cricket—actually a long-horned grasshopper. It was the bane of Utah's first settlers, who in 1848 watched, horrified, as vast "cricket" mobs devoured their crop of ripening winter wheat. Already the Mormons had endured a year of extreme hardship marked by religious persecution and abandonment of their Midwestern homes, the arduous trek west from Illinois, hurried attempts to carve a settlement out of raw desert before the first snows, and a mild but bleak winter of starvation, sickness, and disillusionment. Many survived that initial Utah winter on a diet of thistles, roots, and what deer or wolves they were lucky enough to

Europe. The third (yellow), starting in the late 19th century, spread plague from China as far as the Americas. Today, malaria (green), with its shaking, fever, and chills, has become the world's most prevalent disease. Endemic in the tropics, it afflicts probably 200 million people in Africa alone.

NORTH AMERICA

ATLANTIC OCEAN

SOUTH AMERICA

shoot. And then the crickets began taking the fruits of all their labors, as well as all hope for the colony's success. They grabbed sticks, hoes, rags—anything at hand—to beat back the invaders; they diverted irrigation water to drown them. But the Latter-day Saints were hopelessly outnumbered by this latter-day plague, their wheat doomed. Then, they recorded, a second plague arrived—hundreds of sea gulls (actually California gulls), which the settlers expected would complete the destruction begun by the insects. Instead of going after grain, however, the gulls gobbled up the crickets. Much of the wheat was saved; even more important to the Mormons, confidence in their venture was restored. To this day, the Mormon faithful regard that event in 1848 as an act of Providence; when

it came time for Utah to select an official state bird, the sea gull won wings down.

The crickets, however, would return. Their population still swells and subsides in irregular cycles, and 1985 became Utah's most dramatic "year of the cricket" in nearly half a century. Activity centered in the state's northeastern corner, a lonely and largely treeless realm of hills textured with scattered grasses and sagebrush.

It's the sort of country that shunts the eye away from the near-at-hand and lures it toward the horizon, a land you tend to pass through rather than seek out. Sagebrush all around, stretching to infinity with a grayish green sameness; without really looking at it, you're aware of its small, dark leaves rustling and wiggling. There's a soft, continuous background hiss—like the gentle swishing of weeping willows in a breeze. And then a sudden realization bubbles up into consciousness: *There's not a breath of wind out here.* Your eyes quickly refocus from far to near, and you gape as you realize that not only the sagebrush leaves but also the land itself is crawling with millions of creatures, each the size of a small mouse and as black and angular as Darth Vader. Ominous spikes angle down from the rear of many—mini-cannons, perhaps? They prove instead to be ovipositors, with which females pierce the hard soil at egg-laying time. Each fierce-looking head carries large and complex mandibles, powerful enough to give you a painful nip.

Unlike desert locusts, Mormon crickets cannot fly. They do, however, march in vast, single-minded bands. Step toward them and the hissing you've been hearing crescendoes, as thousands of fleeing crickets sideswipe tens of thousands of sagebrush leaves. Toss a rock into their midst and they undulate outward in concentric rings, like ripples in a pond. Let them be and they soon regroup, continuing their original direction like programmed robots. They are so dedicated to a particular line of travel that witnesses claim to have seen them approach a fence post or telephone pole and, rather than split ranks to go around the obstacle, actually crawl up and over it! When they come upon the unsheltered wilderness of a paved road, those in the lead hesitate, but only briefly; the millions hard on their heels soon force them forward. Vast insect waves then pulse across the highway, ruled by a powerful herd instinct that keeps bands going precisely the same way. How do they choose this common direction, and why do they mass in such numbers?

"Nobody really knows," says Dr. Steven Romney, a Utah entomologist charged with containing several of his area's unwanted insect populations, including Mormon crickets. "They have no demonstrable orientation to the sun, for instance"—as do many other migratory animals. Nor do they seem to rely on a scent trail or prevailing winds. Apparently they sense and follow some signal neither seen, heard, nor smelled by man. Romney has watched cricket bands stretch a mile or two wide and far more in length; crossing one road can take several days. Only a hundred yards to either side of these migrations, though the land appears identical, not a cricket can be found.

"The whole, beautiful thing about this nightmare is that it's a natural cycle," says Romney. "In off years, when crickets aren't in a marauding, expanding stage, you have very timid, solitary individuals. But then something clicks environmentally, possibly even hormonally, that selects for massive reproduction and a high-percentage survival of the offspring."

Just what sets this off isn't known, but Romney suspects a combination of many factors—"physical, chemical, and meteorological." Utah's 1985 plague, he notes, "followed a mild winter with just enough snow to insulate the cricket eggs left in the ground the year before; then a warm, dry

spring with an incredibly warm two weeks in early April; and finally a hot, dry summer. We had all the environmental factors that favor egg hatching and development."

To scientist Romney, the whole plague process is biology on the grand scale, nothing short of elegant. "I'd thoroughly enjoy it if I weren't responsible for killing these suckers," he says with a wry grin. "Every female has the capacity to lay about 150 eggs, so it doesn't take very long to go from solitary crickets to an enormous population. The mathematics is staggering; we don't know if there are billions or trillions. Close to the national debt, probably."

Though plentiful, Utah's crickets of 1985 often proved hard to find and even harder to contain. Infested areas were just too big, the sagebrush cover too dense to spot the insects easily.

"Logistically," explains Romney, "you don't know if you've got an acre of them or three square miles." So his battle plan usually relies on poison-laced molasses bait, sprayed over large acreages in strips or other patterns that afford effective protection with minimal use. Its scent, strongly attractive to crickets, not only fools them into eating a lethal meal but also helps keep them in specific areas. One tract, sprayed only two days earlier, lay black with insect carcasses—one every few inches, uncountable thousands across four or five acres.

Even such dramatic kills, Romney admits, hardly guarantee victory in the cricket war. For although the poison might pack a 95 percent kill rate—considered excellent—it can't match the cricket's high reproductive potential.

"Even if you kill more than 95 percent, you're only just back to where you started—you could still get an equally large population the following season. To really succeed over the long term, you've got to kill every one everywhere." With chemicals, that's simply impossible.

"Crickets are extremely versatile in their diet, doing well on corn, sagebrush, or each other. That's why they're so successful," says Romney, estimating that they eat more than their body weight in a single day, every day. No wonder an invasion of crickets can spark instant alarm in farm areas. "Just last month," says Romney, reminiscing, "I was getting phone call after phone call from people out in Jensen [a small town near the Colorado border], telling me crickets were crossing the Green River. To hear them talk, the crickets might as well have been dinosaurs."

Nor did it help that the gulls and coyotes that year failed to live up to their reputations as cricket killers. Romney believes the celebrated 1848 cricket plague "must have been fairly small, because you'd need a whole lot of gulls to deal with the number of crickets we've got this year."

Heber Thornley, retired state supervisor of grasshopper and cricket control, says, "A lot of people think the gull is the answer to everything. But gulls only show up after the crickets have started swarming and egg laying has begun. So even if they're all eating crickets like crazy, you're still going to have crickets next year."

That's just what happened during the late 1930s and early 1940s, when cricket plagues hit Utah eight years in a row. Heber and his crews—composed largely of Civilian Conservation Corps volunteers—relied mostly on crude, arsenic-based poisons and physical barriers. They strung ten-inch-high strips of galvanized and corrugated metal for miles across Utah's wide-open range, in effect erecting a miniature Great Wall to keep out not barbarian hordes but crickets, which couldn't scale its slick surface. Recalls Heber:

"Every so often we'd make a shallow drop-off. The crickets would hit the barrier and follow it until they reached one of those drop-offs, where they'd fall in and couldn't get out. Of course, the ones behind kept pushing others into it all the time. It's unbelievable how many there could be in a band. They'd just pile up in there by the ton. And stink—the worst stink you could possibly imagine!"

Workers periodically revisited the filled drop-offs to spray them with diesel oil and set them afire, then shovel out the burned carcasses so the pits could refill.

Today's poison-in-the-molasses technique is far more efficient and ecologically sound, since it relies not on contact sprays but on a "stomach poison" that affects only those creatures that actually eat it. Still, it could devastate other mandibular insects, including beneficial ones such as honeybees—and Utah *is* the Beehive State.

Might genetic research some day yield a man-altered bacterium or virus that kills only crickets, thus providing the ideal, poisonless solution? The technology to do so already exists—but costs remain prohibitive, even when compared to this pest's substantial agricultural damages. And there are no guarantees that crickets won't build up resistance to a new microbe almost as soon as it is created.

A third alternative involves reclassifying the cricket from "pest" to "resource" and commercially exploiting it. "It's a good source of protein," says Romney, who suggests the insects be harvested and processed into high-quality animal feeds. "I would think crickets would go over very well in a fish hatchery, say, or as an additive to dog or cat food. It's a matter of taking advantage of a situation." The human food market seems much less promising, although, as Romney points out, there are no apparent biological reasons for people not to eat crickets—only aesthetic ones.

But even if we loved the idea of eating these insects, we'd probably never consume them all. Predation—human or otherwise—simply doesn't work that well on large, plague-type populations. Disease often is a much more effective control, as are stress from overcrowding, failure of food supplies, and other environmental pressures. Cricket plagues, observes Romney, "usually end very abruptly—a snap of the fingers of mother nature" that sends a population plummeting back to normal levels. Again, he stresses, it's all part of a natural cycle; both the insect's periodic blooms and its sudden die-offs stem largely from ecological fluctuations. If man could control just one of these critical parameters—soil humidity or soil temperature, for instance—he could contain their numbers permanently. In fact, one such cricket control has been in limited use for years: turning the soil. Plowing, especially in autumn, says Romney, "brings grasshopper and cricket eggs up to the surface, exposing them both to drying and cold, often killing them outright." The only problem is that most of the American West is not cultivated land but open range, and thus remains a vast and perpetual reservoir of insect eggs, ready for the natural cycle's next upswing.

Crickets and locusts are not only old pests but also endemic ones; they happen to come with certain landscapes and climates. Many other plague creatures are relative newcomers, as much the result of human interference as of natural tenacity. These are the exotics: plants and animals introduced by man into places where they did not previously exist but where conditions enabled them to flourish. History bristles with examples:

Water hyacinth and kudzu both were intentionally introduced into the southern U.S., one for its blossoms, the other as a ground cover for badly eroded soils. Both became pest plants in short order and remain so today.

In 1869, a Harvard astronomer with a side interest in silks brought a European moth species to Massachusetts, in hope of crossbreeding it with Asian silkworms and launching a new textile industry. He should have stuck to stargazing, for some moths escaped, eventually setting off recurrent plagues of what has become the Northeast's worst caterpillar pest—the gypsy moth. This voracious leaf eater can defoliate whole orchards and forests almost overnight; it stripped a record 12.9 million acres of the region in 1981. Years of research and various control techniques—including the introduction of various natural enemies, massive sprayings with DDT and other insecticides, and the development of a synthetic gypsy moth "perfume" that could be used to interrupt normal breeding cycles—all have failed to conquer this pest.

Many other alien insects first reached the U.S. around the last turn of the century, most by accident. Among them:

—the imported red fire ant, an aggressive and venomous South American species now widespread in southern states. Its powerful stings can cause severe irritation and occasionally kill people, and its large dirt mounds can damage farm equipment.

—the fungus-carrying European beetle that spreads Dutch elm disease, a blight deadly to some of our finest native shade trees. Estimated total losses across 30 states have soared to billions of dollars.

—the notorious Japanese beetle, introduced into the eastern U.S. probably in 1911. While never a serious problem in its homeland, it has repeatedly reached plague proportions here, annually costing U.S. agriculture many millions of dollars.

More recent threats include the Mediterranean fruit fly and the African honeybee—the latter intentionally imported to Brazil in the 1950s in hope of breeding a more productive and energetic stock. Now recognized as a major threat to existing honeybee colonies, these so-called killer bees are spreading northward; the alarming news in 1985 that a few had turned up in California left the state's agricultural community buzzing.

Insects have not been America's only pestilential immigrants, of course. Starlings and "pigeons"—more correctly, rock doves—both arrived through the efforts of 19th-century bird-lovers; both became problems in very short order. Starlings flock with native blackbirds and roost in enormous throngs, thousands of them to a single tree. One report from Virginia's Great Dismal Swamp estimated their seasonal numbers at 20 million one year, just within the 164-square-mile refuge. Farmers agonize when such congregations approach, for starlings will ravage fruit, grain, and other crops. Residents worry that the birds and their huge accumulations of droppings might breed disease and potential health hazards. Airline pilots fear even small flocks at airports, knowing that just a few birds sucked into a jet engine can result in flame-out and a crash.

History has shown only too often that we cannot predict all the ramifications of any biological introduction. After sailors inadvertently brought rats to the Hawaiian Islands and the West Indies, 19th-century planters in both island groups imported mongooses in hope of controlling the rodents. Unfortunately, they didn't realize that rats are primarily nocturnal, while mongooses are diurnal—and will dine just as readily on other prey. And so the rat populations fluctuated but never succumbed, as hungry mongooses ravaged native bird and reptile species—often to extinction.

*P*artly to remind them of home, Englishmen took along rabbits when they colonized Australia and New Zealand; this proved disastrous. For although rabbits provided meat, pelts, and sport as well as echoes of the motherland, their legendary knack of procreating soon swelled their numbers far beyond wildest expectations. For one thing, many dry and grassy areas offered ideal rabbit habitat; for another, there were no native predators in New Zealand, while those in Australia had been thinned by farmers. When ferrets, weasels, and stoats, natural enemies of rabbits, were brought from England in hope of exerting some control, they initially had little impact. The bunnies kept on booming—at the expense of native creatures and the land itself.

First introduced in the mid-19th century, the European rabbit reached plague levels in both Australia and New Zealand by the 1880s and 1890s. As early as 1887, Australia's government of New South Wales advertised a prize of £25,000 to anyone who could eradicate this new pest. No one ever collected, but it was not for lack of trying. Traps and poisons were set out; seemingly endless rabbit fences were erected to divide infested areas from clean ones; shooters operated both day and night; more natural predators were bred and released; and burrows were fumigated and dug up. Through it all, the rabbits proliferated. Pastures turned into lunar landscapes; some areas appeared carpeted no longer in grass but in living mounds of gray fur, "as plentiful as ants," according to one report. Graziers grew to hate rabbits far more than eagles or dingoes, since 10 to 15 of them could consume as much forage daily as one sheep.

Help eventually arrived from half the world away in the form of a New World rabbit virus, which proved amazingly lethal to European rabbits. Talk of exporting it to Australia and New Zealand began about 1920, and several introductions occurred in subsequent years, but not until 1950 did it successfully take hold. Transmitted by mosquitoes or occasionally by other native skin-piercing insects, the virus killed Australia's rabbits by the million. Farmers and graziers embraced this new disease—myxomatosis—as a panacea, for the mortality rate among infected rabbits approached 100 percent in 1951; the pests seemed destined for extinction.

With each year of use, however, the virus lost its virulence—while surviving rabbits became increasingly resistant to its effects. The "gray plague" began to rise again. Australians responded by reintroducing the more virulent strains, and by bringing in the European rabbit flea as another vector, or means of spreading the virus from infected to healthy rabbits.

New Zealand, meanwhile, took a different path. Although attempts were made to introduce myxomatosis during the early 1950s, the disease never established itself there. The country continued to develop controls: aerial poisoning, shooting, and trapping, all painstakingly monitored and enforced. It also banned sales of wild rabbit meat and pelts, thus removing an unintentional but long-lived economic incentive that had contributed far more to the rabbit's perpetuation than to its control.

Since the 1960s, New Zealand has reported generally low rabbit densities, now largely maintained by habitat constraints such as reduced cover and high-producing pastures and by predators and disease rather than by human controls. Recently, however, some small areas have suffered heavy rabbit damage, despite the use of control methods that have proved highly effective over most of the country. Some New Zealanders see a final, quick victory with a new weapon: myxomatosis. After all, the virus affects only rabbits, and the proposed vector, the rabbit flea, breeds only on pregnant female rabbits. In heavily infested areas, hefty doses of myxomatosis could produce kills as high as 99 percent and thereafter help maintain low rabbit densities at bargain prices.

The issue, however, is controversial. Some sheep farmers want the virus, while humane societies strongly oppose it. Biologists and other scientists differ as well. Some, including Dr. Michael Godfrey, an ecologist who has served as vertebrate pest scientist at the Invermay research center on New Zealand's South Island, consider myxomatosis only one of several weapons in the anti-rabbit arsenal, and not necessarily the country's best choice for the long run.

Even with spectacular kills, the chances of eliminating rabbits from New Zealand are slim. Outside the small areas of heavy infestation, many rabbits would survive the first round of myxomatosis and would eventually build up resistance to the virus. And, as Godfrey explains, the virus would lose some of its killing power.

"The experience in Australia," says Godfrey, "has been that when you introduce more virulent strains, they don't prevail." Both mosquitoes and fleas transmit intermediate strains more effectively than either very virulent or very weak ones.

The appearance of myxomatosis and the disappearance of large numbers of rabbits, Godfrey warns, could lead to other biological complications. Without rabbits munching on unwanted range weeds, farmers might find themselves devoting a great deal of effort and money to keeping the weeds in check. And without rabbits as a food base, established predator communities would rapidly decline.

When weighing the pros and cons of myxomatosis, New Zealanders must also consider their growing commercial rabbit industry and any possible future uses for the wild rabbit in their country.

"We're talking about introducing a disease and a vector," says Godfrey, "with no way of controlling either. They'd be there, quite possibly, forever."

Compared with some historical pestilences, New Zealand's 100-year rabbit plague seems a mere instant. Consider *the* plague—bubonic plague—whose various epidemics and pandemics gave rise to such nicknames as "Black Death" and "Destroy-ing Angel." To most of the world this deadly sickness, too, is an import. It has traveled from Central Asia in sick rats and their sick fleas, which bite people and inject the bacilli causing the disease. Rats, black and brown, are believed to have originated in Asia. It was man's ships and camel caravans that bore the hitchhiking rodents and fleas around the globe, thereby ensuring plague's eventual ubiquity and prolonged, ever widening epidemics. In return, this unholy trinity of rat, flea, and bacillus has often wrought dramatic changes in human history. Many societies lost a third or a half of their populations, and in such catastrophes law, order, and tradition broke down. Some societies simply collapsed. So did some armies: The pestilence Herodotus credits with killing some 300,000 invading Persians in 480 B.C. may have been bubonic plague; it and the weather helped the Greeks defeat great Xerxes. Similarly, the Roman Empire succumbed not just to barbarian attackers, but also to bubonic plague. All those roads that led to Rome conveyed far more than commerce and military legions. By uniting the empire's capital with its farthest colonies, the ancient world's best highway system also granted ready passage to rats and plague.

The sixth-century "Plague of Justinian," one of several bubonic pandemics, began in Egypt and killed perhaps half the residents—an estimated 100 million souls—in lands around the Mediterranean. Plague also turned back the Fourth Crusade before it reached Jerusalem, and may have afflicted earlier crusades as well. The next pandemic began in Central Asia in the 1340s and raged periodically for 300 years. One of its last surges claimed 70,000 citizens of 17th-century London, mostly in the city's rat-filled tenement areas. It became known not only as the "Great Plague" but also as the "Poor's Plague."

Londoners then did not recognize the role of rats and fleas as sources of the disease—nor would anyone else until nearly the 20th century. For though people noted even in ancient times that large numbers of rats often swarmed in an area during its bouts of plague, they usually assumed the rodents were innocent victims of a human malady, not the cause of its spread. Medieval societies further confused the issue with inconsistencies: At least one army used plague as a form of germ warfare (though germs were yet unknown) by catapulting plague-infected human bodies over enemy walls. Yet the same era produced plague "cures" that included tasting the pus from a victim's open sores, self-flagellation, and leeching. Eau de cologne originated as a protection—totally ineffective, of course—against this disease. Much later, Napoleon, on the move in Italy, dealt with plague in his ranks by having infected men poisoned—or so the story goes.

*T*oday we know to poison rats rather than people, and the horror of plague has faded so much that we tend to consider it part of the distant past, long overcome by medical science. Not so—bubonic plague remains very much with us, and not only in Africa and Asia. One of the largest current repositories of plague, in fact, is the western half of the United States, among ground squirrels and other wild rodents—including prairie dogs, many kinds of rats and mice, and gerbils. This rural plague reservoir is now threatening some of the American West's new suburban developments, next-door neighbors of the infected wild rodents.

Dr. Allan Barnes, chief of the plague branch of the federal Centers for Disease Control, explains that when some western cities expand into ground squirrel country, they unintentionally make finding food and shelter much easier for the rodents. Man-made road cuts and rock-filled erosion barriers, for example, make ideal sites for burrows. So when a city like Albuquerque starts sprawling into nearby foothills, such burrow sites, plus plentiful food, "can increase the number of rock squirrels there four- to eightfold," says Barnes, "greatly increasing the plague hazard."

Over the last decade, 217 Americans are known to have contracted the disease. Not many compared with history's millions, but nearly 20 percent of them died, primarily because diagnosis is difficult in the early and most curable stages, even today. During the same ten years, plague claimed thousands in Africa and Southeast Asia. Though these numbers also represent a huge decrease from past death tolls, Barnes warns that "a plague epidemic can occur if infected rodents come in contact with urban rats and infected fleas pass the bacteria to them."

One complication is that, unlike smallpox or many other plagues of history, bubonic can infect many different animals. Smallpox, for example, involves only man and a particular virus; through inoculation of enough people with an effective vaccine, the disease has been eradicated. But with plague, says Barnes, "we've found it in everything from shrews to camels." Obviously, man cannot inoculate every potential carrier, as he has with smallpox. So the current goal for plague is control, not eradication. Barnes adds:

"To me, plague has the most fascinating ecology of any disease. It's fantastically complex. For one thing, the bacillus is a generalist—it can be transmitted with one degree of efficiency or another by almost any flea in the world."

And by those myriad fleas to a zoo of animals that includes man. Because each species has its own optimal conditions, says Barnes, "just a slight difference in temperature or humidity can alter the possibility of bubonic's transmission by fleas to human beings." Biological, geographical, and ecological variables also play significant roles here, seriously complicating any attempts at predicting plague's next occurrence. In most plague-prone areas, epidemics begin and then cease cyclically—but the cycles are not always regular. In those years when plague is not epidemic, scientists ask, does it live *only* in diseased rodents? Or does it also live in carriers, or even in burrows in the soil?

Where desert locusts went in their off years remained a mystery for millennia, and only some 60 years ago did Boris Uvarov find the solution. Similar enigmas and man's ignorance have fueled all other plagues and pestilences of history. Only after penetrating an epidemic's mystique do we begin to control the epidemic itself. But another baffling affliction always seems to be waiting in the wings. Bubonic plague, yellow fever, typhus, typhoid—these and more have come and gone and come again, like ocean waves. Influenza killed 20 million or more worldwide in 1918-19. In the 1940s and '50s, polio infected 100,000 to 250,000 every year in the U.S. alone until the Salk vaccine stopped the epidemics.

And now there is AIDS—acquired immune deficiency syndrome. First identified in 1981, it already has mushroomed into a twin epidemic: the actual disease, and the fear it breeds. The number of AIDS cases keeps rising; Public Health Service scientists predict that 270,000 Americans will have been afflicted by 1991, and two-thirds of them will have died. The disease's devastating physical effects, its mysterious image, and its relentless nature are so terrifying that newly diagnosed patients often find themselves deserted—even by close friends and family. Telephone callers besiege the Centers for Disease Control and the National Institutes of Health to ask whether avoiding certain restaurants, shops, or public swimming pools will help them evade AIDS. Dentists increasingly wear surgical gloves and masks for routine work. But so far there is no evidence that AIDS can be transmitted through casual contact, such as coughing or sharing, say, an infected person's glass. Indeed, once outside the human body the AIDS virus proves relatively helpless and dies upon drying.

Symptoms of AIDS include severe physical deterioration and weight loss, dementia, swollen lymph nodes, diarrhea, and cancer. The worst effect, however, is the body's growing inability to repel infections, even common ones such as colds or flu.

Roughly half of all AIDS victims succumb to pneumonia, many others to Kaposi's sarcoma, a once rare skin cancer. In fact, they may die of almost any disease, for the virus acts as a biochemical Trojan horse, infiltrating and destroying the body's defenses, thus leaving the door open to infections, some of which are almost always fatal.

Researchers now generally agree that a milder and closely related virus, which infects African green monkeys, mutated when it infected humans, giving rise to deadly virus forms that cause AIDS.

The forms keep changing, and quickly: The AIDS virus mutates at a much faster rate than other viruses. This greatly complicates attempts to devise a vaccine, for even if an antibody could be found tomorrow for today's AIDS virus, a new viral mutation might soon render it useless. So some researchers now are chemically dissecting 20 or so known mutants of the virus, in hope of finding a common region of the protein "envelope" that surrounds the "core" of genetic material in all of them. If they succeed, and can then design an antibody that would attack that particular segment, the antibody should prove effective against all AIDS strains.

A different avenue of research is to create an AIDS "look-alike"—a harmless virus that would possess the same protein coat as the AIDS one. Just as a cousin of smallpox provided an effective vaccine against that disease, the AIDS look-alike would stimulate the body to manufacture antibodies. Then, should AIDS viruses ever invade, the antibodies would "recognize" them by their identical protein coats, be able to attach to them, and destroy them.

Another possibility rests with the discovery of an "on-off switch" that many scientists believe controls the AIDS virus.

FOLLOWING PAGES: Blizzard of migratory grasshoppers descends upon Utah farmer Tim Munns and some recently baled hay. A perennial pest in central and western states, hoppers sometimes undergo sudden population explosions that send their numbers soaring to 100 or even 500 per

Because the virus often remains inactive many years after first invading the body, researchers think it can shift in and out of a dormant phase. If they can decipher the signal, most likely a chemical one, that triggers this apparent shift, they should be able to shut off the virus—for good.

Though a cure has not yet been found, certain drugs offer hope of relieving symptoms and extending lives of AIDS victims. In September 1986 the Public Health Service chose six drugs—AZT, or azidothymidine, among them—for large-scale testing.

Achieving a cure requires complicated, speculative, and costly work. AIDS is a major challenge even for trained scientists with high technology. Invisible except to the electron microscope and unharmed by antibiotics, the AIDS virus seems to have an evil genius. In structural simplicity and operational complexity, it exemplifies nature's inherent elegance. Yet it has no genius, evil or otherwise. It has no brain. The virus is only a mechanism—involved and insidious, but still a mere mechanism.

Ever since man first walked the earth, his mind has enabled him to probe life's mysteries. At first he dealt only with the immediate and obvious; in time he invented myths to explain nature's awesome powers. Gradually he has rejected these creations, as he continues to peel away layer after confusing layer of legend and mystery. With the tools of science, he now has puzzled out many of the mechanisms behind volcanoes and earthquakes, climatic shifts and storms, cholera and smallpox and numerous other biological rampages. Ultimately, AIDS, too, will yield its secrets, as must future plagues that inevitably will arise—plagues and other natural phenomena man has not yet begun to anticipate but will perhaps be less likely to fear.

square yard. Across 10 acres of open range, such concentrations can consume as much forage as 12 or more cows. A warm, dry spring and a hot, dry summer produced the plague of 1985. Billions of insects ravaged millions of acres and cost farmers hundreds of millions of dollars in lost crops and fruit trees. Some Utah residents watched the invaders gobble up all greenery and then start munching the paint off their houses. Recalled one survivor, "It's like being in a horror movie." Or perhaps in a biblical plague: The locust hordes of the Old Testament were a grasshopper species, too.

ERIC BAKKE (FOLLOWING PAGES)

Languishing boxcars on an abandoned rail line near Eufaula, Alabama, slowly disappear under layers of kudzu, an exotic vine that increasingly blankets parts of the Southeast. Introduced into the U.S. in 1876 as decoration in the Japanese pavilion at the Centennial Exposition, this fast-growing

legume at first seemed ideal for preventing erosion and revitalizing depleted soils. While it readily achieved both goals, its 60-foot-a-summer growth has often turned it into a blight—smothering once productive pecan groves (opposite) as well as forests of young pines. Six-foot-deep tuberous roots help kudzu defy weed killers, fire, and plow. Only weeks after burning, vines cover the ground and begin tree climbing (right).

ALL, MIKE CLEMMER

178

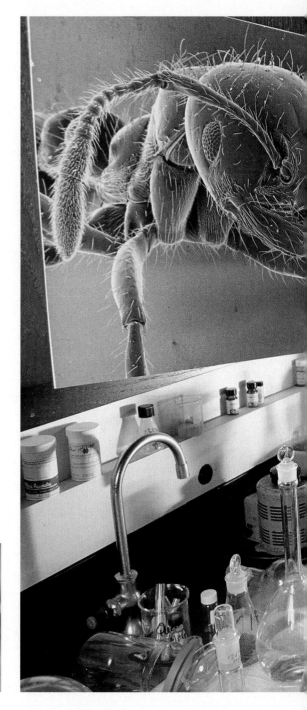

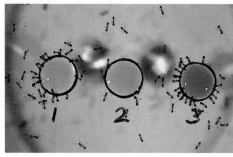

Portrait of the enemy—an imported red fire ant—inspires Texas A & M entomologist Dr. S. Bradleigh Vinson in his search for more varied, effective controls. Appearing in the U.S. in the 1940s, this aggressive Brazilian stinging ant quickly surged across nine southeastern states. Fire ants nest in underground colonies. Because only some ants normally gather food for each colony, Vinson hopes to devise enticing baits containing lethal hormones, fungus, or poisons that these foragers will haul home to their kin. A simple taste test (above, left) compares the relative allure of three baits.

FOLLOWING PAGES: *Fighting fire ants with fire,
Texas ranch hands pour on gasoline—
a one-mound, short-term remedy that cannot
solve a 250-million-acre problem. A larger
one looms: Fire ants have appeared in
supercolonies of connected burrows, with
hundreds of queens and millions of workers.*

Victims of bubonic plague vanish by the cartful into a common grave in a two-century-old engraving, "The Plague Pit." Mass burials were a practical response to the disease's enormous human toll. In just four years, the mid-14th-century pandemic killed perhaps one of every three Europeans.

Clutching a baby's coffin, a grieving woman trudges past a medieval procession of priest and pallbearers. The scene portrays the deadliness of bubonic plague, called the Black Death for the bruiselike skin blotches that foretold imminent death. All wear face scarves to protect themselves from "vapors" they believed could cause the dread disease. Other precautions included self-flagellation to atone for sin, and cologne to combat "bad air." Like many biological scourges, plague spawned intense fears and economic and political chaos, with upheavals that changed whole societies.

E. JENEWEIN

FOLLOWING PAGES: Bubonic plague epidemics struck randomly in Europe for centuries— and death became a popular theme of art. Great and small, rich and poor fell to the killer, as Pieter Bruegel the Elder's 16th-century painting "Triumph of Death" shows in nightmarish detail.

Agents of Black Death: The rat, a flea called Xenopsylla cheopis, *and a bacterium now known as* Yersinia pestis *made a sinister team that eluded human awareness until the turn of this century. Rats such as those foraging in a gutter (below) proliferate in all cities where they find food easily.* Y. pestis *infects rats and other rodents, and the fleas that suck their blood. Sick fleas, their stomachs bloated with bacteria (far right), jump from dying rats onto other animals,*

including people, and inject them with their deadly cargo. The rod-shaped microbes cause plague's swellings of the lymph nodes, particularly in the groin, and also fever, headache, and blood clots under the skin. For millennia, rats with their fleas have stowed away on man's ships, scurried along his trails and roads, and lived in his buildings. Y. pestis *migrated with them, its devastating effects suggested in Old Testament stories, on Babylonian clay tablets, in Homer's account*

of the Trojan War. Throughout history, bubonic plague has exploded periodically. Though quiescent in most parts of the world today, the disease could rage again. Two of the largest reservoirs of Yersinia bacteria live in wild rodents and fleas of the western U.S. and Soviet Central Asia. Contact between these carriers and city rats could lead to epidemics. Vaccines against plague now exist, and antibiotics have been used successfully to treat its victims.

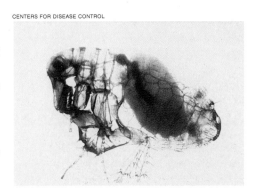

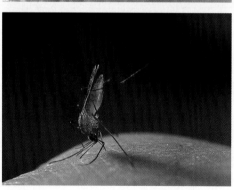

Malaria carrier: A female Anopheles *mosquito plunges its needlelike proboscis into a human finger (above, top) and sucks up protein-rich blood (above, bottom), which will nurture its eggs. With its abdomen distended (large picture), it withdraws. Its saliva prompts the familiar itch—and may*

contain Plasmodium *protozoa. These microscopic parasites eventually infect the body's red blood cells, causing malarial symptoms. The disease spreads to other individuals via mosquitoes. Nearly half the world's population lives in malarial areas, and the disease kills millions each year.*

Microbes and mosquitoes build up resistance
to antimalarial drugs and insecticides,
undermining their effectiveness soon after
they come into widespread use. But genetic
research may soon lead to the creation of
vaccines that someday may help relegate
malaria, like smallpox, to the past.

AIDS—acquired immune deficiency syndrome—challenges Dr. Prem S. Sarin (left), of the National Cancer Institute, and other scientists to find cures and vaccines. The disease ravages the human immune system, brain, and nerves. Death comes within months, chiefly from pneumonia, cancer, bodily wasting, and neurological disorders. The AIDS virus invades T-4 white blood cells that activate the body's natural defenses. It lies dormant in the cells for months or years, during which time the carrier may pass infected T-4 cells to other people. Laboratory tests can identify carriers by the presence of AIDS antibodies in blood samples. Strict precautions protect lab technicians (opposite) from contamination. The virus inside the T-4 cell probably awakens when disease bacteria or viruses alarm the cell into multiplying. But, with the AIDS virus in control of the cell's replication system, only virus copies—or flawed, cancer-causing cell

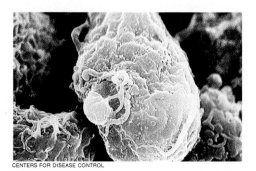

copies—are produced. In the electron-microscope picture above, a new virus buds out of a T-4 cell. By September 1986 the disease had struck some 24,500 Americans, killing more than half of them. The U.S. Public Health Service predicts 270,000 AIDS cases and 179,000 deaths by 1991.

AIDS RESEARCH LABORATORY

AUTHORIZED PERSONNEL ONLY
1. GOWNS MUST BE WORN
2. GLOVES MUST BE USED
3. WASH HANDS

EXPERIMENT

IN PROGRESS

CAUTION

RADIOACTIVE MATERIALS

NATHAN BENN (ABOVE); N.G.S. PHOTOGRAPHER JOSEPH H. BAILEY (FOLLOWING PAGES)

FOLLOWING PAGES: At the Cancer Institute, biologist Daisy Sun carefully withdraws a sample of AIDS-infected cells for drug-effect study. Despite the current rapid rise in numbers of cases, many researchers cautiously predict future victory. Potential cures include creating antibodies capable of capturing any AIDS virus form before it can penetrate white cells. An effective vaccine may come from a naturally harmless AIDS virus that immunizes; or from snipping the reproduction gene from the AIDS virus; or from loading a carrier virus with genes that trigger AIDS-antibody production in people.

193

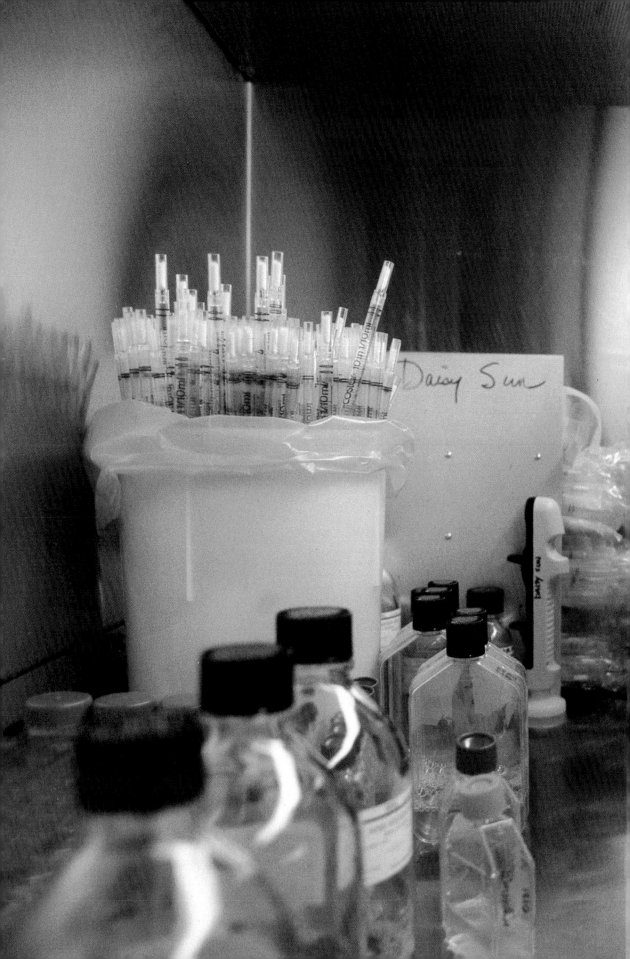

EDI ANN OTTO

UPSWEPT DEBRIS SWIRLS ABOUT A TORNADO IN NORTH DAKOTA.

Notes on Contributors

Born and educated in Iowa, RON FISHER joined the Society's staff in 1962. He has written many chapters for Special Publications and is the author of several National Geographic books, most recently *Our Threatened Inheritance: Natural Treasures of the United States.* While observing the devastation caused by nature's fury in Colombia and Mexico City, Ron noted the spirit of the survivors. "Despite calamity," he says, "people immediately began picking up the pieces and putting their lives back together."

More than 15 years of writing assignments at National Geographic—for the magazine as well as Special Publications—have taken TOM MELHAM around the globe, often in pursuit of natural wonders. He covered earthquakes for *Powers of Nature,* visited arctic wildernesses for *Alaska's Magnificent Parklands,* and explored the world's most spectacular coral reefs for *The Ocean Realm.* Educated in the natural sciences and journalism, Tom has also written a Special Publication on American naturalist John Muir.

Before joining the staff of Special Publications in 1966, CYNTHIA RUSS RAMSAY lived and worked in India and Iran. Over the years she has written chapters for more than a dozen National Geographic books, including *Our Awesome Earth, Alaska's Magnificent Parklands,* and *Splendors of the Past.* "Many assignments expose me to the magic of beautiful places," says Cynthia. "But my research on droughts and floods for this book brought me face-to-face with nature's harsher side and made me aware, as never before, of its mind-boggling complexity."

GENE S. STUART, on the Society's staff since 1978, is the author or co-author of three Special Publications and has written chapters for many others. As a child, she survived a tornado that struck her hometown. She went on to study meteorology at the University of South Carolina and later lived in Mexico. "Corn farmers in our village in Yucatán depended solely upon the rainy season for survival," Gene recalls. "We took part in their rain-god rituals, helped celebrate their harvest, and one year witnessed their suffering and resignation when the rains never came."

Acknowledgments

The Special Publications Division is grateful to the individuals and organizations named or quoted in the text and to those cited here for their generous assistance during the preparation of this book: Nicholas Ambraseys, Richard Andre, Richard Andrews, Margaret Anstee, Richard L. Armstrong, Newman Bolls, Edward Braithwood, William J. Brennan, Fernando Caracena, Bob Case, Mehmet Celebi, Lawrence C. Childs, A. M. Choudhury, William Craven, Jr., Dick DeAngelis, John W. Everest, Bill Ewart, Kerryn Frecker, Jeffrey A. Gritzner, Peter Hammond, Nicholas A. Hopkins, John Hotard, Walter Howard, David Jimenez, J. Kathryn Josserand, Fred Koch, Harry Koundakjian, Miles Lawrence, Barry Longridge, Nancie J. Majkowski, Bernard Nahlen, National Earthquake Information Center/USGS, Sharon Nicholson, David A. Nickle, Elizabeth A. Nielsen, Richard Orville, George Pararas-Carayannis, Bart Peerbolte, Waverly Person, Donald W. Peterson, Carolyn Z. Roth, Robert Sheets, Haraldur Sigurdsson, Steven H. Singer, B. F. Smith, Peter B. Stifel, William C. Stone, Carl von Hake, Randy White, Mike Wiegele, J. Morgan Williams, Stanley Williams, Don H. Wood, Donald E. Wuerch.

Additional Reading

Readers may wish to consult the *National Geographic Index* for related articles and books. Pertinent periodicals include *Earthquake Information Bulletin* (U.S. Geological Survey), *Mariners Weather Log* (National Oceanic and Atmospheric Administration), and *Weatherwise* (Helen Dwight Reid Educational Foundation / American Meteorological Society). The following books may also prove helpful: CHAPTER 1: Ian Burton, Robert W. Kates, and Gilbert F. White, *The Environment as Hazard;* Kendrick Frazier, *The Violent Face of Nature;* W. M. S. Russell, *Man, Nature and History;* Anders Wijkman and Lloyd Timberlake, *Natural disasters: Acts of God or acts of Man?* CHAPTER 2: Robert Decker and Barbara Decker, *Volcanoes;* Douglas Myles, *The Great Waves: Tsunami;* Time-Life Books, *Earthquake* and *Volcano.* CHAPTER 3: Reid A. Bryson and Thomas J. Murray, *Climates of Hunger;* Patrick Hughes, *American Weather Stories;* Cecil Woodham-Smith, *The Great Hunger;* Donald Worster, *Dust Bowl: The Southern Plains in the 1930s* (Oxford University Press). CHAPTER 4: Richard A. Anthes, *Tropical Cyclones: Their Evolution, Structure and Effects;* Roger G. Barry and Richard J. Chorley, *Atmosphere, Weather & Climate;* Joe R. Eagleman, *Severe and Unusual Weather;* Martin A. Uman, *Understanding Lightning.* CHAPTER 5: Stanley Baron, *The Desert Locust;* J. L. Cloudsley-Thompson, *Insects and History;* Charles S. Elton, *The Ecology of Invasions by Plants and Animals;* Robert Hendrickson, *More Cunning Than Man: A Social History of Rats and Men;* William H. McNeill, *Plagues and Peoples;* Geoffrey Marks and William K. Beatty, *Epidemics.*

Index

Library of Congress ⬚ Data

Nature on the rampage.

   Bibliography: p.
   Includes index.
   1. Natural disasters—Popular works. I. National Geographic Society (U.S.). Special Publications Division.
GB5018.N37 1986 904'.5 86-21865
ISBN 0-87044-587-1 (regular edition)
ISBN 0-87044-592-8 (library edition)

Composition for *Nature on the Rampage* by National Geographic's Photographic Services, Carl M. Shrader, Director, Lawrence F. Ludwig, Assistant Director. Set in Zapf International. Printed and bound by Holladay-Tyler Printing Corp., Rockville, Md. Film preparation by Catherine Cooke Studio, Inc., New York, N.Y. Color separations by the Lanman Progressive Company, Washington, D.C.; Lincoln Graphics, Inc., Cherry Hill, N.J.; and NEC, Inc., Nashville, Tenn.